LANGLEY ADAMS LIBRARY

May 2008

SPORTING TRADITIONS

Since 1856

BEGINNER'S GUIDE TO

Bird

WATCHING

Creative Publishing international

Creative Publishing international, Inc.
400 First Avenue North
Suite 300
Minneapolis, MN 55401
1-800-328-3895
www.creativepub.com
All rights reserved

President/CEO: Ken Fund
VP for Sales & Marketing: Peter Ackroyd
Publisher: Bryan Trandem
Acquisitions Editor: Barbara Harold
Production Managers: Laura Hokkanen, Linda Halls
Creative Director: Michele Lanci-Altomare
Senior Design Manager: Brad Springer
Design Manager: Jon Simpson

Band-f Ltd President: f-stop Fitzgerald
Development Director: Karen Jones
Production Director: Mie Kingsley
Book Design: David Perry
Production: Stephanie Lora
Director of Photography: Bruce Curtis
Select photographs from this book are available via our websites,
www.band-f.com or www.f-stopfitzgerald.com

Library of Congress Cataloging-in-Publication Data

King, Alicia.
The ORVIS Beginner's Guide to Birdwatching / Alicia King
p. cm.
Includes index.
ISBN-13: 978-1-58923-349-2 (soft cover)
ISBN-10: 1-58923-349-2 (soft cover)
1. Bird watching. I. Title.

QL677.5.C77 2007
598.072'34--dc22   2007010817

Printed in Singapore
10 9 8 7 6 5 4 3 2 1

ORVIS®
SPORTING TRADITIONS
Since 1856

BEGINNER'S
GUIDE TO
Bird
WATCHING

BY **ALICIA KING**

FOREWORD BY **PERK PERKINS**

PREFACE BY **SCOTT WEIDENSAUL**

PHOTOGRAPHY BY BRUCE CURTIS AND F-STOP FITZGERALD

Creative Publishing
international

Produced by BAND-F Ltd.

CONTENTS

PART TWO: GETTING THE MOST OUT OF BIRDING

PART THREE: THE NEXT STEPS

FOREWORD

PERSONAL REFLECTIONS ON BIRDS
AS OUR CONNECTION TO THE NATURAL WORLD
BY PERK PERKINS

I have been a passionate birder my whole life, thanks to my father, Leigh H. Perkins. He made sure that I experienced, early on, the many joys of this unique hobby. As outdoor activities go, birding is special, particularly for newcomers. It can be enjoyed everywhere and anywhere. There is no need to outfit yourself with a lot of fancy equipment, and all that is necessary to get started is your curiosity, a binocular, and a field guide. Once you are hooked, however, you'll never be far from your binocular. I keep one in my car and make sure I pack one for all my travels.

In buying this book, you have already decided to take up birding. We welcome you to the club. While there are many excellent sources of information available, such as detailed field guides, nature centers, and bird organization web sites, this book has been written just for you, the beginner. It has all the information you need to get started, and then some. Even a seasoned birder like me has picked up many helpful hints.

I wish you a terrific time in getting to know the birds who share our planet. Remember there are a lot of them out there, so set reasonable goals. Meanwhile, you will be surprised at how quickly you learn the basics, and how much enjoyment you will derive from birding.

PREFACE

EVERYTHING YOU NEED TO KNOW TO ENTER THE EXCITING WORLD OF BIRDWATCHING
BY SCOTT WEIDENSAUL

The best way to introduce you to this wonderful hobby is to reveal its well kept secret… birdwatching is fun!

If you are just getting into birding (or birdwatching—take your pick) the explanations that Alicia King offers in this handy volume will ease your way into one of the most rewarding pastimes imaginable.

Birdwatching is one of the fastest-growing pursuits in the United States; the federal government says there are now more than 46 million Americans who watch and feed birds and, for more than a decade, the hobby's growth has outpaced virtually every other form of outdoor recreation.

Why? It's inexpensive, easy, and exciting, but the best reasons are the birds themselves. There are birds found everywhere you look, from varied thrushes and hermit warblers singing in conifer forests of the Pacific Northwest, to cactus wrens and hummingbirds of the desert Southwest. From the hordes of wading birds in Florida to the springtime flush of songbirds across the Eastern woodlands. From snowcapped

TOP: KNOWN FOR ITS YELLOW FEET AND BLACK LEGS, THE SNOWY EGRET FEEDS IN SHALLOW WATERS WITH A DIET MAINLY OF FISH AND WATER INSECTS. BOTTOM RIGHT: PERSONALIZING BIRDHOUSES MAKES A UNIQUE BACKYARD STATEMENT. BOTTOM LEFT: BIRDWATCHING IS A HOBBY THAT ANYONE CAN ENJOY.

mountains to the open ocean, there is no habitat without colorful, active, and melodic birds.

Birdwatching is also the most portable hobby in the world; all you need are eyes and ears. In fact, thanks to the globe-girdling phenomenon of migration, a world of birds comes through our backyards twice each year, uniting the Arctic and the tropics and everything in between. In spring, a walk each morning through a familiar park or around the neighborhood is a treasure hunt for the newest travelers to drop in—tanagers on their way back from Mexico or the Andes, warblers from the Greater Antilles, vireos from the Amazon. It is never the same cast of characters twice.

Being a birder can be as simple or as complicated as you want to make it; it can be something you do puttering around in your backyard, a competitive sport, a portal to conservation, or a reason to travel the globe. It can be, and for most birders is, all of these things.

If only I'd had a book like this when I was starting out as a birdwatcher almost forty years ago, learning by trial and error. I didn't know how to pick good binoculars or choose a field guide. With Alicia King's expert guidance, you'll learn what took many of us years to figure out—how to find birds, what to wear, where to go. She will help you figure out the gadgets and gizmos that will make birding more efficient and enjoyable. She suggests birding hotspots around the country and gives tips on how to track

BIRDWATCHING IS THE MOST PORTABLE HOBBY IN THE WORLD; ALL YOU NEED ARE EYES AND EARS.

your sightings; she takes the mystery out of bird identification.

She also explains how to take your hobby to the next level, including "extreme birding" events like the annual World Series of Birding, a 24-hour team marathon that pits many of the best birders in the world against each other in an intense, but friendly competition that raises millions of dollars for conservation.

Finally—and perhaps most important—she explains how you can use your newly found enthusiasm to save the birds themselves. With solid information on conservation, including groups that are working to preserve birds and bird habitat, she tells you how to make this a better world for birds.

So grab your binocular, head outside, and look up. There's a world of delight and surprise waiting out there.

INTRODUCTION

WELCOME TO THE JOYS OF BIRDING
BY ALICIA KING

I have always enjoyed watching birds—even before I really knew that much about them. I didn't even know my enjoyment of them had a name: Birdwatching. Of course I knew I was watching birds, but didn't realize it was considered a sport or something that would generate so much interest among so many people. According to the U.S. Fish & Wildlife Service National Impacts of Wildlife Viewing Survey, millions of people participate in wildlife viewing, with the majority of those considering themselves to be birdwatchers, also known as birders.

Birds are beautiful to watch. They make an incredible variety of songs, sounds, and calls. They exhibit fascinating behavior and come in all shapes, sizes, and colors. Birds range in size from small hummingbirds with relatively small wingspans to the California condor with a wingspan exceeding 9 feet (2.7 m). Sandhill cranes stand over 4 feet (1.2 m) tall and have incredibly long legs. A wren has a small body, short stubby tail, and very small legs. A roseate spoonbill has a bill

THE VARIOUS JOYS OF BIRDING: TOP LEFT: IT ALL BEGINS WITH AN EGG. TOP RIGHT: THE MIGHTY OSPREY APPROACHES ITS NEST. BOTTOM RIGHT: A PEACEFUL HABITAT CAN YIELD MANY SIGHTINGS. BOTTOM LEFT: THE EVER-POPULAR AMERICAN ROBIN SNAGS A MEAL.

shaped like a spoon, and a long-billed cur-lew has a long bill that curves downward.

The individual characteristics of birds show nature's diversity in all its glory. Birds embody the freedom we humans can only dream about. They are beautiful and exotic—a living fantasy. Whether I am watching pigeons in a local park, hawks perched on trees on the side of the road, or the American eagle soaring overhead, I find birds absolutely fascinating. The sheer variety of birds in our world amazes me.

When I think of birds, I think immediately of the romance of their flight. They go wherever they want, whenever they choose, some at incredible speeds. I can imagine the world through the eyes of a bird while it is soaring above the earth. However, a bird's life is not an easy one and is filled with the tasks necessary for survival: looking for food, searching for places to rest, and watching for predators.

A lot of people seem to be under the impression that birdwatching is only for seniors. My preteen daughter and teenage stepson would disagree. Our family has spent a lot of our time, and many holidays, watching birds. It is just something we do. It is a little hard not to watch birds; they are all around us. Whether we spend our time working in the yard, hiking, kayaking, visiting nature centers, camping, or taking a simple walk in the woods, we are always prepared to watch birds. Sometimes we take trips to find birds.

It is exciting to watch a flock of sandhill cranes during their migration. They fly on the thermals high in the sky and sometimes circle as they ride. Sometimes you can hear them in the sky before you see them. These huge birds dangle their legs as they descend from the sky, calling to each other. This usually happens at dusk as they gather by the hundreds or thousands at certain locations. Once on land they interact by calling, nipping at each other, and doing a "dance" where they raise their wings and necks and let out the most incredible trumpeting sounds. I make a point of going to watch this every year, especially in the fall. I will talk more about migration routes, stopover points, plus the eating and roosting habits of the sandhill cranes, so you can travel to see this magnificent event.

Throughout the years I have learned a lot about birds, their habitat, and their behavior. The more I learn, the more I want to know and the better I become at identifying them. This book is designed to give you, the reader, an overview of the world of birds and how to identify and learn more about them.

Whether you are a beginning birder, an intermediate birder, or even an experienced birder, I hope that as you move through the chapters you gain a better understanding of birds, their lives, and the role they play in our lives. I will take you through the first phase of getting started, giving you what you need to know and to do in order to get the most pleasure out of birdwatching.

I hope you enjoy reading this book as much as I have enjoyed writing it. Delight in the wonder of birds and share the joy of birdwatching with others.

Let's get started.

PART I
GETTING STARTED

CHAPTER ONE

BIRDWATCHING BASICS
BE PART OF THE EXCITING WORLD
OF BIRDWATCHING

- *Key benefits of birding*

- *Birdwatching in a group*

- *Tips for successful birdwatching*

Birdwatching, also known as birding, is something that can be done alone, with family members, with friends, or within a group. No matter the level of expertise, anyone can go birdwatching, and whether you can identify birds or not, you can still consider yourself a birdwatcher. However, it is much more fun when you begin to learn more about them.

KEY BENEFITS OF BIRDING

Once you start learning how to identify birds, you will notice them in surprising places. Recently, I was walking downtown in a city and noticed a vacant lot that had been planted with a variety of trees, flowering bushes, and plants. There were a number of birds: warblers, sparrows, a few goldfinches, and a handful of cardinals. On a nice spring day this park would be a great place for people to gather to watch the birds. When you think about how much of a city is paved, it is nice to see a place where birds can find a haven.

During fall and spring migrations, birds often fly above or through cities. Having these little spots of greenery can be helpful

TOP LEFT: BIRDING IN A GROUP CAN BE A VERY EDUCATIONAL EXPERIENCE. TOP RIGHT: HARRIS' HAWK IS A DESERT AND BRUSH COUNTRY DWELLER SEEN MAINLY IN TEXAS AND ARIZONA. BOTTOM RIGHT: FAMILY ACTIVITIES CAN INCLUDE SEARCHING THE SKIES FOR UNFAMILIAR BIRDS. BOTTOM LEFT: THE COSCOROBA SWAN, FROM SOUTH AMERICA, IS THE WORLD'S SMALLEST SWAN.

to the birds plus offer a place for people to relax. The daily grind keeps us busy, and when a place to enjoy nature and watch birds can be provided, it is a very welcome relief.

Birdwatching can be therapeutic. I frequently hear people say that a walk in the woods, watching and listening to birds and other nature sounds is very relaxing. There seems to be a countrywide trend of creating habitats in backyards so people can have a sanctuary where they can retreat at the end of the day. Many offices and schools are setting up feeders so everyone can enjoy birds during the work day, as well.

Learning what birds eat, where they bathe, and where they build their nests and raise their young will help you create a habitat to bring them into your own sanctuary. I will talk more about creating habitats and feeding birds to get the most enjoyment out of watching them in your backyard in Chapter Three.

Learning about the different families of birds, their shapes and sizes, their colors, their field marks, and the habitats they prefer, makes identifying birds easier and more rewarding. It is an accomplishment to be able to name a bird you've been watching for a while.

Everyone in the family can participate in birdwatching, and I consider it a lifelong adventure. I took my daughter on her first official walk when she was barely four weeks

THE NORTHERN MOCKINGBIRD SOMETIMES SINGS ALL NIGHT LONG DURING NESTING SEASON.

old. She wasn't old enough to really birdwatch herself, but the point is that I shared the experience of being outdoors and watching birds with her as she grew up. She started asking if we could go for walks, and she would point out the birds as she saw them.

You can learn a lot from other people while you are watching birds. However, don't let other birders intimidate you. No one was born with all the knowledge of a birder. They had to learn just like you.

Some people learn very fast and others, like me, take a little longer. The advantage of birding alone is that you can take your time and look things up and think about what you are watching without feeling like you are holding a group back. The advantage of birding with just friends or family is that they will usually wait for you. The disadvantage is that you don't have the collective knowledge of many experienced birders in a birding group.

THE WHITE PELICAN HAS A WING SPAN OF ABOUT 9 FEET (2.7M). IT CATCHES FISH BY SWIMMING ON THE SURFACE OF THE WATER AND SCOOPING THEM UP WITH ITS BILL.

REWARDS OF BIRDING

Whether you decide to go birdwatching with your family or in an organized group, there are many benefits. Watching with family members or friends enables you to share the activity and learn together. Birding with a group also often results in new friends and new experiences. You have the opportunity to learn a lot about the birds you are watching, especially when the participants have a variety of birdwatching skill levels. This gives you the freedom to watch, learn, ask questions, and experience watching birds in a way that can help you build your own skill level.

BIRDWATCHING IN A GROUP

There are a lot of organized birdwatching opportunities. Many nature centers schedule bird walks with naturalists or volunteers to lead the group. Local bird clubs and Audubon Societies typically organize walks at parks or plan field trips to places known for good birding. These organized walks offer the opportunity to learn more about identifying birds because the leaders of the trip and participants are usually experienced birdwatchers. They focus on areas during the peak time of bird activity, such as migration.

While the biggest advantage of birding in a group of birdwatchers is that you can benefit from their collective knowledge, there are a few disadvantages. Sometimes groups are on a tight schedule and rush through a bird walk to be sure to make it back on time. Sometimes when you are in a large group you may miss a bird if the bird flies away before you get near it. I like to take my time and really watch the birds and their behavior. Being in a group where people rush through just to add a bird to their bird list doesn't add to my enjoyment of the hobby. In most cases when I am in a group, I have fun because of the diversity of the people. I learn from watching and talking to others, and I enjoy the company of people who, like me, enjoy watching birds.

Birdwatchers observe birds with the naked eye, or through binoculars, scopes, or cameras. Most birdwatchers pursue their hobby for recreational or social reasons. They listen, watch, and learn about birds. Their passion sometimes translates into feeding birds, creating backyard

THE RANGE OF THE BLACK-CROWNED NIGHT HERON INCLUDES FIVE CONTINENTS WITH A LARGE POPULATION IN NORTH AMERICA. JUVENILES ARE STOCKY AND HAVE A YELLOW BILL.

habitats for birds, studying birds, or caring for birds through conservation actions.

There are casual birders, beginning birders, intermediate birders, and hard core birders. Some participate in citizen science; they study birds for school, or study or work with birds as part of their profession. Then there are people—you may be one of them—who like watching birds but don't make a big deal out of it.

Casual birders often love watching birds in their own backyard, on a simple walk through a park, or along a trail. Most people, young and old, are casual birdwatchers without even realizing they are watching birds. They typically don't take binoculars or field guides on their walks, but if a book or guide is available they may look up a bird to find its name.

The beginning birder is one who has just started birding and knows enough to identify the basic birds yet they may not be able to name them. The American robin is a bird that most people recognize by sight, yet some couldn't tell you it is called a robin. A beginner is often eager to learn the names of birds and how to identify them. They also take the next step of going on a local bird club trip. They may purchase a field guide or also invest in a simple binocular. I will talk more about field guides and equipment in Chapter Six.

Intermediate birders typically spend more time in the field looking for birds and will participate in field trips to specific areas to watch for certain birds. They can recognize birds by size, colors, and field markings, and can name the majority of them. Intermediate birders will

WATCHING BIRDS WITH OTHERS IS A FUN AND REWARDING ACTIVITY.

WHAT DOES A BIRDWATCHER DO?

One of the great things about birdwatching is that you can do it almost anywhere. I have taken my family on many trips, and even when we are kayaking or hiking, we watch birds. When we are sitting in an outdoor restaurant, we watch for birds. Walking through the parking lot on the way to the mall or the baseball game, we scan the skies for birds. Sometimes the kids will give me a look as if to say "Come on mom, lets go," but they always stop and look with me. Whether you are in your own backyard, a shopping center, a ball game, a local park, or a national park or refuge, birds are almost everywhere.

start to become more serious about learning birdsongs and calls and will spend more time gaining knowledge about birds. Intermediate birders also read magazine articles about birds or about places to watch birds. They enjoy getting more involved in the hobby.

Hard core birdwatchers take themselves very seriously and spend a lot of money and time devoted to the sport. They also travel great distances to watch birds, often dropping whatever they are doing to search for a rare bird. Most of these birders have multiple bird lists and some like to keep lists of birds they see divided by state, national park or refuge, country, or year. I will talk more about life lists and other bird lists in Chapter Six.

Hard core birders seem to eat, sleep, and drink birds. They buy the most up-to-date equipment and spend a lot of hours in the field hunting for a new bird to add to their life list. They seek out places where they can find birds they haven't seen before, and will connect with other birders to be sure they don't miss a potential bird sighting. They stay on top of the various birding listserves, and read the latest magazine articles.

Birdwatchers, whether casual, beginner, intermediate, or hard core, can participate in citizen science projects. These projects vary in degree of difficulty, but most are fun and easy. A lot of them can be done as a family or even with a classroom. Ornithologists, however, are engaged in the formal scientific study of birds for specific research or conservation reasons. I spend a lot of my time reading journals, research papers, and citizen science program reports associated with bird

YOU CAN LEARN A LOT BY BIRDWATCHING WITH OTHER MORE EXPERIENCED BIRDERS.

conservation. I will talk more about these projects in Chapter Nine.

I believe that anyone who watches birds, no matter the level of expertise, is a birdwatcher. The more you do it and the more you learn, the more you will enjoy it.

TIPS FOR SUCCESSFUL BIRDWATCHING

There are a lot of things you can do to make sure you have a good time while birding. My biggest tip is to have fun. Birds are amazing creatures and when you take some time to learn more about them, the more rewarding birding becomes. I never force my family to endure a birding trip if they don't want to go along. Our children—my husband's son and my daughter—enjoy spending time with us, and we always watch for birds wherever we are.

Below is a list of several of the most important tips I can share. For many of the tips there is more detailed information in subsequent chapters.

Be Comfortable

- Wear comfortable clothes and dress for the weather. Nothing spoils a trip faster than not being prepared. Dress in layers so you can adjust your temperature.
- Try not to wear clothes that crinkle and make noise as you walk. You want to make as little noise as possible.
- Try not to wear bright clothes. They make your presence too obvious. This rule applies unless you want to attract hummingbirds. I once wore a red scarf around my neck and hummingbirds kept buzzing me as I walked along. I guess they thought I was a really big flower.
- Wear comfortable shoes. Consider where you are going to walk and wear shoes that will handle a wet path or rocky terrain. You don't have to wear hiking boots, but sturdy, comfortable shoes are a must.
- Wear sunscreen or protective clothing and hat. Even if the sun is not out in full force, or it is a cloudy day, you will still be exposed.

EVERYONE IN THE FAMILY CAN PARTICIPATE IN BIRDWATCHING.

THE GREAT BLUE HERON IS THE LARGEST HERON IN NORTH AMERICA. IT IS OFTEN SEEN STANDING AND HUNTING FOR FISH ALONG THE EDGES OF PONDS AND RIVERS.

- Wear bug protection. Depending on where you are birdwatching, bugs can be a problem. I once went on a trip and was pleasantly surprised there were no mosquitoes, so I left the bug repellent and long-sleeved shirt behind. That was a mistake; later on the trip the bugs were thick and relentless. I was scratching my bites for the rest of the week-long trip.

Choose Your Birding Time and Place
- You will find that most birds are more active in the early morning, and then again in the early evening hours. This is the time birds are actively feeding.

FORMERLY CALLED THE SPARROW HAWK, THE AMERICAN KESTREL IS ONLY SLIGHTLY LARGER THAN A ROBIN.

- Walk facing away from the sun. Looking into the sun to watch birds makes it hard to see them. The light distorts their size, shape, and color.
- Consider a place that has an easy path or trail system. This way you can focus on birding and not worry about getting lost or trying to remember which way to go. As you start to bird more, you will find places that offer longer trails.
- Consider joining a bird club or nature center that has regularly scheduled walks. This will increase your chances of seeing some birds, and you will have some help identifying them. These types of walks are typically scheduled for weekend mornings. Keep your eye out for calendars of events that list walks or bird hikes. They often advertise a variety of nature activities and events like owl walks—usually held in the late evening—which can be quite fun.

Do a Little Homework
- If you have chosen a nature center or place to walk that has a visitor center or bulletin board, take a minute to check out their bird list. Many times people post a list of birds they have seen. If you can't find one, stop and ask what birds have been seen recently. This will give you an idea of what to look for or which birds you might have a chance to find.
- If you have an idea of the birds found in an area where you plan

to watch, check a field guide so you can see what they look like.

- Check the weather forecast. Don't let potential rain or wind catch you off guard.

Take the Right Equipment

- Take a field guide with you. Don't constantly look at the book while in the field, but have one handy so you can look up interesting birds. In Chapter Ten I will talk about how to choose a field guide.
- Carry a binocular. Binoculars are designed to enhance your birding experience, not inhibit it. Don't get frustrated by them. If you find that you are spending a lot of time learning to focus, stop using them. Have fun walking and seeing the birds that are easy to see. Once you are home again, you can learn how to operate them. See Chapter Six for more about binoculars and other optics.
- Include a bird checklist or a notebook so you can be sure to keep track of the birds you see.

Practice Makes Perfect

- Relax and take your time. You will see a lot more birds if you stroll quietly.
- Stop every once in a while to look and listen. You will see birds that you may have missed while you were walking.
- Learn how to "pish." Pishing is the ability to purse your lips and produce a sound that can attract birds. Chickadees

BARN SWALLOWS MAKE THEIR NESTS IN MAN-MADE STRUCTURES, SUCH AS BRIDGES AND BARNS.

and titmice seem to be attracted to this sound. Birds will come close to see what the noise is all about.

- Don't try to learn everything at once. Focus on familiar birds that you see regularly. Once you master these, you can start looking at families of birds. You will have an easier time identifying them if you understand how birds are related and what characteristics make them unique.
- Practice. Even experts continue to improve their skills. The more you bird, the better you become and the more fun you will have.

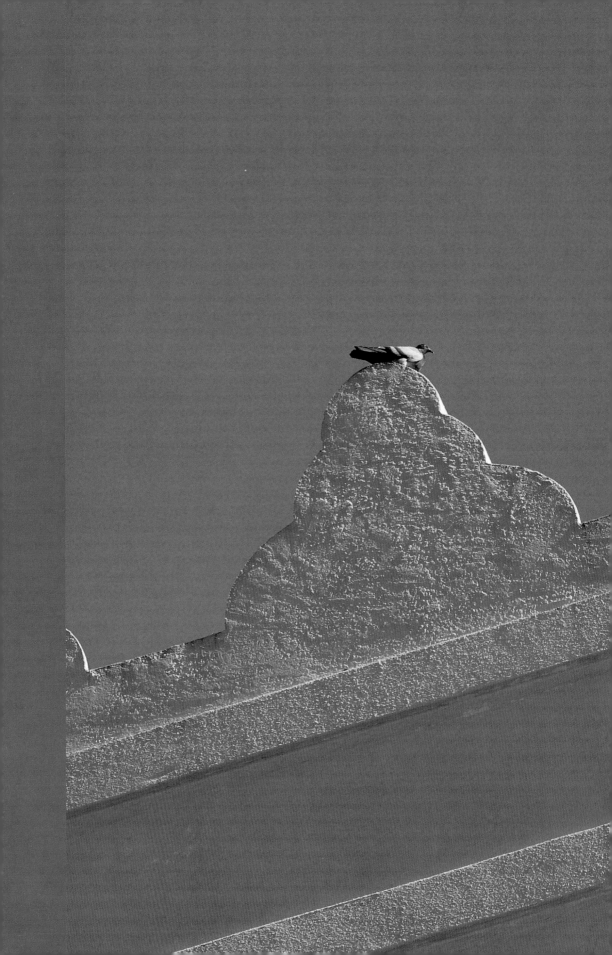

CHAPTER TWO

FIRST THINGS FIRST: GETTING STARTED

EVERYTHING THE BEGINNER NEEDS TO KNOW TO LAUNCH A BIRDWATCHING CAREER

- *Basics of birdwatching*

- *The right time and place*

- *The right equipment*

- *Using a field guide*

- *Courtesy counts*

Identifying birds can be extremely frustrating to beginning birdwatchers, especially when a bird flashes in front of them and they can't focus their binocular on it. For this reason, many people give up before they get a good start.

Practice and patience will allow you to identify birds in the field more easily. Identifying birds doesn't need to be hard. This is a fun hobby, filled with exciting opportunities to see birds and learn about the species that surround you. There are several things to keep in mind as you start watching birds.

BASICS OF BIRDWATCHING

First, it is easier to learn how to identify birds if you reduce the number of choices you have. In most cases you can ask the local nature center or bird club what the most common birds in your area are, or what other locales feature. Your field guide will provide the basic information needed to figure out what they look like, what habitat they are most likely to be found in, and what family they belong to. Once you know the top ten to twenty birds in your area, start reading up on them.

Knowing the different common birds will help you identify them. You also want to get a basic understanding of what a hummingbird, a robin, or a jay is. In addition to making a list of the most common birds in your area, research birds you are less likely to see. Go through your field guide and put an "X" next to birds that may not typically occur in your geographic area. For example, in the western states there are only a few places where you are likely to see the Mexican jay. Focus on the most common jays in your area and start to memorize them. In most of eastern North America, there is only one type of hummingbird that occurs regularly, the ruby-throated hummingbird. While several other hummingbirds have been seen, why worry about trying to identify uncommon birds until you have more

FIELD GUIDES WILL HELP DEVELOP YOUR EXPERTISE ABOUT THE BIRDS YOU ENCOUNTER.

IDENTIFYING BIRDS

Learning about the sizes and shapes of birds can help you learn to identify them. Take a look at the overall shape. Don't get too caught up on size as it can be a little misleading depending on how far away the bird is. Look at the shape of the head of the bird—does it have a crest or is it rounded or flat? Is the bill pointed, thick or blunt, long or short? Are the wings long or short, wide or narrow, or pointed or rounded? Is the tail forked, long, or broad? When you start to put all the answers to these questions together, you may find that you can get pretty close to identifying the bird you see flying or perched, even if you can't see the color very well.

THE COMMON YELLOWTHROAT IS SEEN FROM COAST TO COAST, OFTEN IN WETLANDS WITH REEDS OR CATTAILS.

experience with the most common species of hummingbird?

Consider the time of year the birds are present. Are they found year-round in your area, just during migration, or during spring, summer, or fall? You can reduce the number of birds you have to worry about identifying if you make a list of the birds you will most likely see.

As you try to identify a bird look for the following: the bird's shape and size; its color and field marks; its behavior; its habitat preferences; and its voice. This may seem like a large amount of information to gather, but you often need only one or two of these clues to identify a bird.

Birders ask: Is the bird the size of a sparrow, the size of a robin, or the size of a crow? What is the shape of the bird? Does it have a long tail, a short tail, long wings, a long or short bill? What color is the bird? All one color, banded, striped, wing bars? Where is the bird? Is it on the ground, in a bush, in a wooded area, or a pond? How is the bird behaving? Is it flitting around catching insects, hopping on the ground, or flying overhead? Is it singing? What does it sound like? As your birding abilities increase, you will be able to pinpoint the important clues with greater ease and confidence.

Sometimes birds are not always easy to identify. If you are watching a bird in low light or when the sun is behind the bird, it may be hard to see its true colors. Size can also be difficult to judge if the bird is some distance away from you. There also may be a lot of variation between male, female, and young birds. Birds may also have different-colored plumage in spring and fall. The more clues you can consider when looking at the bird, the easier birding will become.

THE RIGHT TIME AND PLACE

Most birders go in the early morning or evening when birds tend to be most visible and active. However, the best time of day to birdwatch depends on what birds you want to see, the season, where you are geographically, and the weather. A lot of birds are not very active during the middle of the day, especially in the hot summer months. If you want to catch a few owls or nighthawks, late evening is best.

In North America, spring is a terrific time of year because most birds tend to be

THE MALE INDIGO BUNTING PRESENTS A BRILLIANT BLUE COLOR, WHILE THE FEMALES ARE A DRAB BROWN.

very colorful and active then. Using the local nature center, wildlife refuge, or bird club is a good way to figure out what species may be around at any time of year. Bird listserves can also be helpful, particularly during spring migration

Most birders enjoy birdwatching year-round and focus on specific species, tracking their migration and patterns of movement. Some birds migrate long distances and others' movements are short and sporadic. Some birds don't migrate at all but may move depending on weather and other circumstances. Learning when and where birds move will help you determine when is the best time of year to go birding for specific species. Once you start watching birds you will see them in many places you never noticed before. You may find yourself taking your binocular with you just in case. I own several binoculars and keep one in my car, one by the kitchen window, and one in my backpack. Everyone in the family has their own pair so I don't have to worry about sharing mine.

Beginners can start in their own backyard, neighborhood, local city and state parks, greenways, or converted rails to trails, which are old railroad beds that have been turned into hiking and bike trails. More options could include the local sewage and holding ponds, shopping centers, a sod farm, or maybe the local dump.

Learning the habits and habitats of the birds will help you decide when and where to watch them. The following is a reference guide to help you find the most common birds in the most common habitats. It also comments

Top left: Most preserves and parks offer birding opportunities year-round. Top right: Laughing gulls are well named because of their characteristic laughing call. Bottom right: The cactus wren is the state bird of Arizona. Bottom left: The mournful cooing of the mourning dove is a familiar sound in many neighborhoods.

on where in the habitat you are likely to find this bird, and any helpful behavior traits.

Urban and Rural Backyards and Parks

Starting in your backyard is probably the easiest way to build basic birdwatching skills. If your neighborhood is full of yards that are grass lawns with little or no native plants or water sources, the birds may be limited. You will probably still see some basic birds, such as sparrows, jays, American robins, and blackbirds or crows, even if the habitat is not the best. English house sparrows are in city backyards, parks, and in habitats that include buildings and shopping centers. Take a close

REFERRING TO YOUR FIELD GUIDE AFTER YOU HAVE CAREFULLY STUDIED A BIRD HELPS PERFECT YOUR IDENTIFICATION SKILLS.

FIELD GUIDE BASICS

All field guides are designed to help you identify the birds by using photos or pictures with descriptions of the birds' shapes, sizes, and field marks. They also provide sound clues, habitat descriptions, and maps of their range. It is helpful to know the seasons and locations so by process of elimination you can narrow the choice of birds you may have seen. Keep watching the bird as long as you can and remember as many features as possible; you can always refer to the guide later. The more practice you get watching the birds, the better you will become at identifying them faster the next time.

look at these sparrows and think about how they look, how they behave, and their size. As you watch other birds, you will want to compare the size of this bird with them.

Many suburban and urban birds tend to be very adaptable. City and suburban backyards can be homes to robins, jays, cardinals, sparrows, and mockingbirds, as well as many other songbirds. In addition to the typical yard birds, many city parks are good for some owls and birds of prey. Especially in the winter, Cooper's hawks can be seen hunting for small prey. They have been known to stalk songbirds at feeders. See Chapter Three for more on feeders.

Some parks are very small parcels of land, and others are very large. Many of them create an "edge effect" where you can find a nice variety of birds. This edge effect is when there is a mix of habitats, an area where the woods or hedgerow meets a meadow or field.

If you want a good look at a Canada goose, a city park may be a great place to observe this bird. They are relatively easy to identify and observe. Because they are usually on an open pond or grassy area around a pond, you can take some time to watch them and get to know their behavior and their field marks. Sometimes you will be rewarded with a great blue heron or other water birds.

State Parks

State Parks can offer great birding habitats. Most have been created to provide recreational opportunities such as camping, fishing, hiking, and overall wildlife and nature

THERE ARE FEW BIRDS MORE FRIENDLY THAN THE BLACK-CAPPED CHICKADEE. AT FEEDING STATIONS, MANY BECOME TAME AND ACCEPT FOOD FROM OUTSTRETCHED HANDS.

enjoyment. The habitats vary depending on the geographical terrain of the state. They are often equipped with a nature center and a staff dedicated to helping visitors enjoy the wildlife. Regular nature or bird walks are frequently offered and can provide a chance to learn more about area birds. Most state parks post bird sightings at the nature center so you have a good reference of what to look for as you explore the park.

National Parks and Provincial Parks

National and provincial parks provide habitat critical to many species of migratory and nesting birds—from raptors and shorebirds to songbirds. Varying from arctic tundra to tropical rainforests, they are among the best places to watch birds, and they provide critical breeding,

THE ROSEATE SPOONBILL IS NAMED FOR ITS SPOON-SHAPED BILL, AND HAS GORGEOUS ROSE-COLORED FEATHERS.

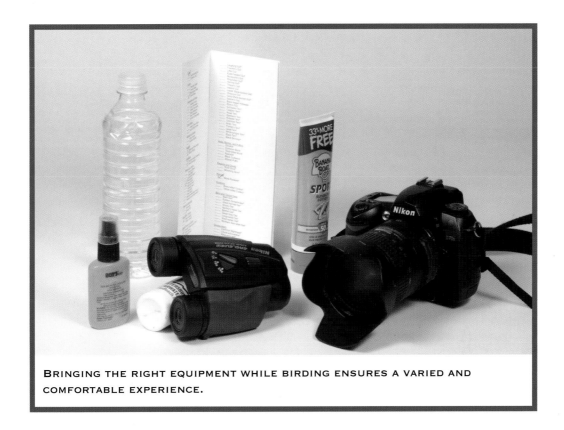

BRINGING THE RIGHT EQUIPMENT WHILE BIRDING ENSURES A VARIED AND COMFORTABLE EXPERIENCE.

migratory stopover, and wintering habitats. Many parks have been designated as "Globally Important Bird Areas" by conservation organizations. These areas are not only extremely important for birds, they are also a birdwatchers' haven during spring and fall migration.

National Wildlife Refuges

In the United States, national wildlife refuges are home to more than 700 species of birds. Many wildlife refuges were established primarily to provide feeding, resting, and nesting habitat for migratory birds. Each year they are used by millions of migrating birds. Many of the refuge habitats provide shelter for a variety of species including neotropical migratory birds, raptors, mammals, and endangered species.

THE RIGHT EQUIPMENT

While you don't need anything special to go birdwatching, having the right equipment can help make your adventure more fun and enjoyable. What I take depends on where I am going, how long I will be there, and the weather prediction. I always layer my clothing, for example, and having the right binocular can make it easier to see and identify birds.

This is what I usually take on a quick birdwatching trip:

Backpack with:

- Water bottle. I always take one no matter where I go or how long I will be gone.
- Binocular with a strap. Get the binocular harness strap because it is less irritating on the neck and more evenly distributes the

SINGING SWEETLY FROM DAWN TO DUSK,
THE WESTERN-WOOD PEWEE FEEDS ALMOST
ENTIRELY ON INSECTS.

weight of the binocular. Bring a Lens Pen to clean the lenses.

- Field guide. I like Kenn Kaufman's *Field Guide* as a quick reference.
- Notebook and pencil. I use the weather-proof Rite in the Rain notepads (www. riteintherain.com).
- Insect repellent, rain jacket and hat.

Being physically comfortable is important and wearing good shoes is key. Walking shoes or tennis shoes are often fine for an easy walk. If you know you are going someplace with a rough terrain, hiking boots or heavy-duty shoes are best. In cold weather or in areas where you know you will be exposed to water, consider winter boots or water waders. Gore-tex boots and shoes are waterproof and still breathe. Wool socks with a liner of silk or polypro will help wick away the moisture, keep your feet dry, and reduce blistering. Happy feet make for a happy birder.

Birding vests come in all sorts of styles and are very handy. I like being able to free myself of having to carry a pack every time I bird. The average vest has multiple pockets designed to carry a variety of tools you may need. There is a pocket for a notepad and pencil, a place for a packet of tissues, and a pocket for a Lens Pen and more. I like the pocket vests that give easy access to a field guide and also have a spot for a rain jacket. There are a variety of vests available at sporting goods or specialty stores and online at birding websites.

Packs can be found in almost any store. Be sure to get a pack that will easily hold your gear and fit on your back or around your waist comfortably. An outside pocket or two will allow you to fetch items without rummaging around the bottom of the pack. I like a pocket to hold my water bottle and my field guide. The American Bird Conservancy's *All the Birds of North America* field guide is tall and thin, so it fits easily in a side pocket or even a pant leg pocket. Packs should be a neutral color so they don't attract too much attention.

SOME SPECIAL AREAS AND TREES ARE SET ASIDE FOR THREATENED AND ENDANGERED BIRDS TO NEST IN. IT IS BEST NOT TO DISTURB THEM.

PROPER BIRDING ETIQUETTE

American Birding Association's Code of Birding Ethics provides a guideline for most birders to follow. The complete list of the Code of Ethics begins on page 46. Below are the basic rules:

- Be respectful of wildlife and its environment.
- Avoid stressing birds or exposing them to danger; exercise restraint and caution during observation.
- Keep away from nests and nesting colonies, roosts, and important feeding sites.
- Stay on roads, trails, and paths where they exist; otherwise, keep habitat disturbance to a minimum.

- Respect the law and the rights of others.
- Do not enter private property without the owner's explicit permission.
- Follow all laws, rules, and regulations governing use of roads and public areas, both at home and abroad.
- If you are attracting birds to an area, ensure the birds are not exposed to predation from cats and other domestic animals, or by dangers posed by artificial hazards.

ABA CODE OF BIRDING ETHICS

Most birders use the American Birding Association "Code of Birding Ethics" as a guide to ethical birding. It is printed here in its entirety.

1. Promote the welfare of birds and their environment.

1(a) Support the protection of important bird habitat.

1(b) To avoid stressing birds or exposing them to danger, exercise restraint and caution during observation, photography, sound recording, or filming.

Limit the use of recordings and other methods of attracting birds, and never use such methods in heavily birded areas, or for attracting any species that is Threatened, Endangered, or of Special Concern, or is rare in your local area;

Keep well back from nests and nesting colonies, roosts, display areas, and important feeding sites. In such sensitive areas, if there is a need for extended observation, photography, filming, or recording, try to use a blind or hide, and take advantage of natural cover.

Use artificial light sparingly for filming or photography, especially for close-ups.

1(c) Before advertising the presence of a rare bird, evaluate the potential for disturbance to the bird, its surroundings, and other people in the area, and proceed only if access can be controlled, disturbance minimized, and permission has been obtained from private landowners. The sites of rare nesting birds should be divulged only to the proper conservation authorities.

1(d) Stay on roads, trails, and paths where they exist; otherwise keep habitat disturbance to a minimum.

2. Respect the law, and the rights of others.

2(a) Do not enter private property without the owner's explicit permission.

2(b) Follow all laws, rules, and regulations governing use of roads and public areas, both at home and abroad.

2(c) Practice common courtesy in contacts with other people. Your exemplary behavior will generate goodwill with birders and non-birders alike.

3. Ensure that feeders, nest structures, and other artificial bird environments are safe.

3(a) Keep dispensers, water, and food clean, and free of decay or disease. It is important to feed birds continually during harsh weather.

3(b) Maintain and clean nest structures regularly.

3(c) If you are attracting birds to an area, ensure the birds are not exposed to predation from cats and other domestic animals, or dangers posed by artificial hazards.

4. Group birding, whether organized or impromptu, requires special care. Each individual in the group, in addition to the obligations spelled out in Items #1 and #2, has responsibilities as a Group Member.

4(a) Respect the interests, rights, and skills of fellow birders, as well as people participating in other legitimate outdoor activities. Freely share your knowledge and experience, except where code **1(c)** applies. Be especially helpful to beginning birders.

4(b) If you witness unethical birding behavior, assess the situation, and intervene if you think it prudent. When interceding, inform the person(s) of the inappropriate action, and attempt, within reason, to have it stopped. If the behavior continues, document it, and notify appropriate individuals or organizations.

Group Leader Responsibilities

4(c) Be an exemplary ethical role model for the group. Teach through word and example.

4(d) Keep groups to a size that limits impact on the environment, and does not interfere with others using the same area.

4(e) Ensure everyone in the group knows of and practices this code.

4(f) Learn and inform the group of any special circumstances applicable to the areas being visited (e.g., no tape recorders allowed).

4(g) Acknowledge that professional tour companies bear a special responsibility to place the welfare of birds and the benefits of public knowledge ahead of the company's commercial interests. Ideally, leaders should keep track of tour sightings, document unusual occurrences, and submit records to appropriate organizations.

Reprinted with permission of the American Birding Association **www.americanbirding.org**

USING A FIELD GUIDE

A field guide is a book designed to help the reader identify birds, and is an essential component of birdwatching. They are typically small enough to carry into the field and inexpensive enough that almost anybody can purchase one. Field guides contain pictures, range maps, descriptions of habitats, migration patterns, and the calls and songs of most of the birds in the book. Field guides are an invaluable tool for birders.

All birds have unique physical traits such as shape, color, and field marks. These field marks, combined with other clues such as habitat distribution, voice, and behavior, helps you identify birds. Roger Tory Peterson invented the field guide in the 1920s. Peterson used artist-illustrated birds with arrows pointing out the field marks so birders could learn what is important for identification.

Field guides contain pictures of birds that are either photographs or illustrations—the one exception to this is the Kaufman *Field Guide,* which uses a digitally enhanced photograph. Field guides with photographs show actual birds as photographed by professional nature photographers. The disadvantage of photos is that the bird images are taken under conditions—light, weather, season—which may be different from those when you are seeing the bird. Guides with illustrations mean you are not seeing an actual bird, but an artist's rendering of one.

FIELD GUIDES ARE AVAILABLE IN A WIDE VARIETY OF FORMATS.

The advantage of these guides is that the birds' characteristics can be illustrated better to help you pinpoint what to look for.

Purchase a field guide that is appropriate for the region where you live or where you want to watch birds. There are field guides for all of North America; for just the eastern or western half; for specific states or provinces; and for smaller geographic areas, birding trails, and specific refuges or parks.

Field guides come in a variety of shapes and sizes. You should choose one that you find easy to use and to carry in the field. If a field guide is too large or heavy, you may find that you won't use it as much. Save the larger, more extensive field guide or reference book for further research at home.

Take a little time to look over the field guide and familiarize yourself with how it is arranged. Field guides are typically organized taxonomically. This means that related birds are grouped together. This taxonomical order has been established by ornithologists and goes from the least-evolved birds—loons, grebes, waterfowl—to the most highly evolved birds—warblers, sparrows, finches. Some field guides provide a color-tab key to help you find bird families quickly.

The following are some of the most widely used field guides. Take some time to explore the field guides at your local bookstore, library, or nature center. Don't be afraid to ask others why they like their field guide. I own all of the guides listed below and like to use them all at some point or another. I keep them in my car,

IT MAY COME AS A SURPRISE BUT CITY PARKS OFFER TERRIFIC OPPORTUNITIES FOR BIRDWATCHING.

TOP LEFT: THE GREAT CRESTED FLYCATCHER IS MORE EASILY HEARD THAN SEEN. TOP RIGHT: WILD TURKEYS HAVE BEEN REINTRODUCED INTO MANY AREAS OF NORTH AMERICA AND CAN BE VERY STRONG FLYERS. BOTTOM RIGHT: WELL-MARKED TRAILS ARE A BIRDER'S PARADISE. BOTTOM LEFT: WOOD THRUSHES HAVE A BEAUTIFUL SONG AND HAVE EARNED THE NAME "THE FLUTE OF THE FOREST."

my kitchen, family room, and in my backpack so I can run out the door quickly for an impromptu birdwatching trip.

ONE OF THE MOST COMMON NORTH AMERICAN WOODPECKERS, THE NORTHERN FLICKER DIGS INTO THE GROUND TO FIND ITS PREFERRED FOOD, ANTS.

All the Birds of North America

This guide covers all the birds of North America and has instantly-observable characteristics. The range maps are small and not the easiest for discerning the boundaries of the birds, but it is easy to use and fits nicely in a pant or vest pocket.

Audubon Field Guide to Eastern Birds in North America and *Audubon Field Guide to Western Birds in North America*

This all-photographic field guide describes species found in the western or eastern regions of North America. It features full-color, high-quality nature photographs and a detailed range map for each species. This guide groups the birds by color and shape.

Golden Field Guide A Guide to Field Identification of Birds of North America

This guide covers all the birds of North America in one volume and is small enough to fit in a pocket. Range maps are adjacent to the text and opposite the pictures of the birds, which is helpful when verifying the habitat of the birds.

Kaufman Field Guide to Birds of North America

Using digitally enhanced photos rather than drawings, this guide makes it very easy for a beginning birdwatcher to recognize the birds seen in the field. The guide is organized by bird family groupings rather than strict taxonomic classification. The text and maps for each species appear on the same page as the images, though the maps are small and it is sometimes hard to distinguish the regions.

National Geographic Field Guide to the Birds of North America

This guide illustrates more than 800 North American bird species. The birds are described with range maps on the same page as the bird illustrations. A large field guide but easy enough to take in the field.

SPRING IS A WONDERFUL TIME TO WATCH BIRDS; THEIR COLORS ARE BRIGHT AND THEY SING UP A STORM.

Peterson, A Field Guide to the Birds East of the Rockies

The *Peterson Field Guide Series* features all birds of eastern and central North America, shown in full color and described in detail. The field marks unique to each bird are pinpointed.

The Sibley Guide to Birds

The *Sibley Guide* covers all of North America. Although this guide is too heavy and large to carry in the field, its depictions of birds are extremely realistic. For the 810 species covered in the guide, there are more than 6,600 painted illustrations—with variations of male, female, and juveniles, as well as breeding and non-breeding plumages. Every bird is shown in flight. This is a great book to have as a reference after a birding trip in the field.

COURTESY COUNTS

The most important thing to do while birding, other than having fun, is to be respectful of the people and wildlife around you. Obey all signs and rules posted or written about an area. Rules typically include: stay on the path, don't chase or flush wildlife, don't litter, and don't disturb others. If you are on a guided tour at a nature center or park, the leaders of the walk will usually define the rules before you go.

I lead a lot of walks with school groups, scout troops, and families, and sometimes have more trouble with the parents than with the children. I tell people to keep their conversations to a minimum as the talking will decrease our chances of seeing birds. I request that if people see a bird that I miss, they should raise their hand and call out the bird name softly if they know it. More often than not, people do have a clue as to what kind of bird they are seeing and can call out "there's a hawk" or "there's a sparrow" even if they don't know the proper name.

I have to remind people to turn off their cell phones or to mute them. However, these days more birders not only use their phones to stay in touch with their family or business, but they also may use their cell phones to let people know where the birds are or what they are seeing. Some birders use two-way radios or walkie-talkies to communicate to each other. If you choose to use a cell phone or radio, be mindful of the group—check with the leader to make sure it is okay. Sometimes the noise can be a signal to the bird that there is a disturbance and this may limit the birds that you see. Some birds may move closer to see what the sound is. Chickadees and titmice are notorious for this. In most cases, it is best to stay quiet. If you must have gadgets, keep them for the times you are birding alone or when the group okays their use.

The quieter and more unobtrusive you are, the more birds you will probably see. It is always okay to talk softly or ask questions, but be careful to choose the right times. It is not the right time to ask to borrow something from someone when a bird has come into sight and everyone is looking at it.

It is always important to be sure you stay on the trails and don't trespass on private property. Get permission from the owner of a property if you want to bird there. Some nature centers, national wildlife refuges, and national parks or sanctuaries have areas that are off-limits to visitors. While these may seem like great spots to bird they are off-limits for a reason. The National Wildlife Refuge in Wisconsin is an example. There are several areas that are closed to visitors because of the habitat restoration work for red-headed woodpeckers. There is also an area in Necedah where the endangered whooping cranes are housed during the spring and summer, before their flight south for the winter. The Whooping Crane Eastern Partnership raises the cranes from eggs taken from captive birds. Because they have no natural parents, they are taught how to fly and later how to migrate. The birds learn to follow ultralight airplanes flown by costumed Operation Migration team members. In the fall, the birds follow the planes south to Florida. Once in Florida, the whooping cranes spend the winter there and fly back to Necedah in the spring. This area of the refuge where they live and are trained is off-limits to visitors because contact with humans could jeopardize the project and cause harm to the birds.

It is also important to remember not to stress any birds. Be cautious when you observe or photograph them. Stay clear of obvious nests and young birds. If you see a bird is building a nest or feeding young, watch from a distance. If a bird appears to be stressed, back off even farther. Give animals their space; you may unknowingly invite predators to the bird's nest by getting too close.

CHAPTER THREE

BACKYARD BIRDING

SOME OF THE BEST BIRDWATCHING MAY
BE RIGHT OUTSIDE YOUR WINDOW

- *Is your backyard bird friendly?*

- *Types of bird feeders and birdseeds*

- *Making water available*

- *Creating a habitat*

- *Protecting your backyard birds*

- *Watch out for windows*

- *Orphan birds*

Attracting birds to your backyard is a great way to see birds up close and learn more about them. Once you start to identify the birds you see on a regular basis, you will feel more confident about identifying them in other places. Plus, having birds right in your backyard to enjoy will provide great entertainment for you and your family.

IS YOUR BACKYARD
BIRD FRIENDLY?

Does your backyard attract many birds? If not, there are a variety of things you can do to invite them into your yard. Along with birds, you will also attract butterflies and beneficial insects. You can create a bird friendly habitat no matter what size your yard. A bird friendly habitat is a combination of food,

HAVING FEEDERS IN YOUR YARD IS A GREAT WAY TO GET UP CLOSE AND PERSONAL WITH THE MANY BIRDS THAT WILL VISIT THEM, SUCH AS THESE HOUSE SPARROWS.

FEEDER CARE

Feeding stations may be an important factor in a bird's well-being. Poorly maintained feeding stations may contribute to the occurrence of infectious disease and mortality. By taking some simple steps, you can prevent or minimize problems at your feeders.

- Use a good seed or blend or other food type. Discard any food that smells musty, is wet, or looks moldy.
- Keep the feeder area clean of waste food and droppings. Raking or shoveling the discarded seeds and seed hulls can help keep the area clean.

- Avoid overcrowding by providing ample space between feeders. Crowding can create stress which may make birds more vulnerable to illness or predators.
- Provide cover about 10 feet (3 m) from feeders so birds can flee predators such as cats or hawks.
- Clean and disinfect feeders regularly. Disinfect with one part household bleach in nine parts of water—a 10 percent solution. Rinse the feeders completely and allow to air dry.

water, shelter, and places for birds to raise their young. Providing all the components of a habitat can ensure that your sanctuary will attract a variety of birds.

Food for birds can include bird feeders in addition to trees, shrubs, and other plants. The plants in your yard can provide food, shelter, and nesting sites. Nesting boxes can be added to improve the habitat. Add a birdbath for water, and you've covered all the elements needed. Once you've created a suitable habitat, you will be amazed at the birds that visit your backyard.

TYPES OF BIRD FEEDERS AND BIRDSEEDS

Feeding birds can be as simple as placing a handful of seeds in a dish on a deck rail, or filling a feeder and waiting for them to find it. Birds generally find their food by sight, so placing your feeder where it will be visible should increase their ability to see the food. Sprinkling some seeds on the ground or on top of the feeder is a good way of letting birds know that the feeder has food.

The feeders and seeds you choose will help determine the bird species you attract. Different birds eat different seeds and foods; you will want to take some time to figure out who is already visiting your yard and who you want to invite.

There are several feeding behaviors that birds exhibit while choosing what they eat and where they feed. Some birds feed on the ground, and others will eat on a feeder placed on a pole with a wide perching area. Some birds will feed from a feeder that

MAKE SURE YOU CHOOSE THE RIGHT KIND OF BIRDSEED FOR THE BIRDS YOU ATTRACT.

swings in a breeze and others will cling upside down to feed.

Feeders come in a wide variety of styles. There are hopper (wood) feeders, platform feeders, suet feeders, tube feeders, and specialty feeders designed to supply specific bird food. The average tube, platform, or hopper feeder is designed to hold oil sunflower seeds, or a blend of seeds to feed birds like cardinals, chickadees, and titmice. A tube feeder with very small holes is designed to hold nyjer (thistle seed) for goldfinches and other birds with small bills. Suet feeders hold suet (rendered beef fat) to feed insect-eating birds such as woodpeckers. A specialty feeder for hummingbirds holds a nectar solution. A feeder that only allows for upside down-feeding will attract

TOP: THE BRIGHT RED FLOWERS OF
THE ROSE-OF-SHARON TREE ARE
A BEACON FOR HUMMINGBIRDS.
BOTTOM: THE VIVID SCARLET
COLOR OF THE MALE CARDINAL IS A
COMMON SIGHT AT FEEDERS.

specific birds like woodpeckers, nuthatches, and other clinging birds, but will not feed birds like cardinals, doves, and sparrows.

The best seed to start feeding birds is oil sunflower seed. All seed-eating birds will eat it. It fits in most tube feeders and in hopper and platform feeders. There are also feed socks and wire feeders that hang to accommodate oil sunflower seeds for birds. Birds will perch on a tube feeder or the sides of a wood or platform feeder to access the seed. Most birds will break the sunflower seed open to eat the meat inside. Chickadees and nuthatches will fly in to a feeder to choose a seed and then fly away to break open the seed somewhere else. Chickadees crack the seed open with their beaks while holding it with their feet.

Oil sunflower seed will attract cardinals. These birds generally eat on the ground but will come to a wood or platform feeder as well as a tube feeder. Cardinals will fly in to a feeder and typically sit at the feeder to eat the seed. They roll the seed around in their beaks, break the seed open, eat the meat, and spit the seed hulls out.

Most ground-feeding birds seem to prefer millet and seeds like sunflower. Using a tray feeder with a blend can accommodate both elevated and ground-feeding birds. Birds up at the feeder will eat the larger seeds, such as sunflower and safflower, while those at the ground level will eat the millet that falls to the ground.

The more variety you supply, the larger the variety of birds you will attract. Diversity is the key, but watch what feeders and seeds you provide. Cheap feeders may not last long and may be harder to clean. Cheap seed may seem attractive at the time, but in the long run, much of it may be wasted and cost you more.

The common varieties of food in bird feeders are seeds, nuts, suet, nectar, and fruit. Black-oil sunflower seed has a high fat content and its small size and thin shell make it easy for small birds to crack open. Sunflower seeds can be placed in wood feeders, platform, tube feeders, or wire feeders designed with holes large enough for birds to pull the seed out.

Striped sunflower is another birdseed that a lot of seed-eating birds will eat, though the hull is larger and thicker than oil sunflower seeds and can be a little harder for some birds to open. Jays and titmice seem to be attracted to striped sunflower seeds. Striped sunflower seeds can be placed in almost all feeders that use oil sunflower seeds.

Thistle (or nyjer) seed is imported from India and Ethiopia, and attracts finches including American goldfinch, pine siskin, and common redpoll. Nyjer seed is used in a feeder specifically designed for the smaller-billed birds. Sometimes finches are picky eaters. It may take them a while to get used to coming to your new feeder. Check the seed in the tube by shaking it every once in a while to be sure that the seed is not moist. If so, or if a month or two has passed, replace the seed. Be patient, it is worth the wait!

Safflower looks a lot like sunflower seed. It has a bit of a bitter taste, and while cardinals and other big-billed birds will eat it, most birds seem to prefer sunflower seeds over safflower. Because of its bitter taste, it is also a seed used to keep squirrels and blackbirds away from the feeder.

Millet is a small, round grain and is commonly used in seed mixes, and is a favored food of smaller, ground-feeding birds such as doves, juncos, and sparrows. It is often added

PROVIDING FEEDERS IN YOUR BACKYARD IS A GOOD WAY TO ATTRACT BIRDS.

to seed blends and can be placed directly in a platform feeder low to the ground.

Milo is also added to some seed blends, but unfortunately it is not eaten by most birds, and often goes to waste. In the west, some birds will eat it, but in the east, very few do.

Most birdseeds can be mixed together and placed in a feeder to attract a variety of birds. High-quality blends may contain sunflower, safflower, and some millet. Some mixes may also contain milo, cracked corn, and other grains. Less expensive brands may contain larger amounts of "filler" seeds (like milo or wheat)—these should be avoided. A blend high in oil sunflower is always a better choice in seed blends.

Peanuts are a great additional food to offer your backyard birds. High in protein and oil content, peanuts attract titmice, jays, and woodpeckers. Peanuts should be served roasted and without added salt. When placed in a cage feeder or added to a seed blend, the peanuts should be shelled. Left in the shell, peanuts can be strung together and birds will hang on the string to break the meat out of the shell.

Suet is a good choice of energy-rich food for attracting insect-eating birds such as nuthatches, chickadees, and woodpeckers. Most suet is beef kidney fat that has been rendered and re-solidified into cakes. This process keeps the suet from melting in warm climates. Suet is also available at many butcher counters, but you would want to be sure to change it frequently. Suet can also be purchased as processed cake that includes seeds, berries, and other ingredients. Be careful if you offer suet in hot weather; it may become rancid if it has not been specially processed. Suet is typically offered in cage-like containers hung from trees or next to other feeders.

Hummingbirds feed mostly on insects and will visit flowers for their nectar. The sugar-water blend placed in special hummingbird feeders mimics the natural substance produced by flowers. You can purchase commercial nectar preparations, or you can make your own by simply mixing one part sugar to four parts water. Boil the water, then add the sugar. Let cool and fill the feeder. Keep hummingbird feeders clean; change the solution about every three days to prevent mold and deadly fermentation. You can store extra sugar water in your refrigerator for up to one week. There is no need to add red food coloring to nectar, and it might be harmful to the birds. Red feeders or red portals on the feeder, or even a red ribbon tied on it will help attract the birds. Never use honey or artificial sweeteners. Honey grows mold that can be harmful to hummingbirds.

Fruit draws many bird species and makes a great addition to backyard bird feeding. Grapes and raisins will attract mockingbirds and robins, while orioles and catbirds will eat grape jelly. Orange halves offered on a tray feeder or nailed to a tree or feeder can attract a number of bird species, including woodpeckers and orioles. Though their main diet is insects, bluebirds will also eat raisins, nut meats, sunflower chips, and meal worms.

THE SOUND OF RUNNING WATER IS A SURE WAY TO BRING BIRDS TO YOUR HABITAT.

ATTRACT BIRDS WITH WATER

Water is one of the easiest and least expensive ways to attract a variety of birds to your backyard. Water can be provided in a simple dish on the ground, such as a saucer from under a potted plant or an old Frisbee, or in an elaborate fountain. The sight and sound of moving water seems especially attractive to birds, so if you can add a dripper or mister to even the simplest of baths, you will likely attract birds. Water is an important ingredient in your backyard habitat and taking care of the placement of the bath will help keep the birds safe. Place the bath in an open area that has some shelter within about 10 feet (3m) or so. This shelter can provide a safe place for birds to dry off and preen and also escape predators if need be.

least 20 minutes at 250°F (121°C). Crush them into pieces no larger than sunflower seeds. Offer them in a low platform feeder, separate from your other feeders.

Birds don't depend on feeders for their primary source of food. While it is nice to provide them with a regular supply of food, they will not starve if you do not feed them. You can go on holiday and the birds will find other food sources and be back later to check out your feeder. You may, however, find it harder to attract them back if you have left your feeders empty for a long period of time.

If you have not yet been feeding birds in your backyard, it may take days or months before the birds in your area discover your new feeder. Be patient and you are sure to be rewarded. There may also be situations that exist in your yard that may increase or decrease the enjoyment you receive from feeding the birds. Squirrels or birds such as pigeons or blackbirds, may be hogging the feeder. Birds may be scared off by house cats and birds of prey while trying to feed. Don't be shy about exploring your options and trying new things. Have fun watching all the great birds you will attract to your yard!

MAKING WATER AVAILABLE

Birds need clean water for drinking and bathing. A dependable source of water will attract birds and keep them coming to your yard. The sound and sight of water dripping or gurgling will attract a variety of birds and can be entertaining to watch. You can provide a simple source of water for birds by

BIRDS ARE EASILY DRAWN TO THE SIGHT AND SOUND OF MOVING WATER.

Birds have muscular, stomach-like gizzards that "chew" their food. To aid in this process, birds swallow small, hard materials such as sand or small pebbles. They will also "eat" other sources of grit such as eggshells or ground oyster shells. Grit can be added to your feeder station and purchased at most wild bird-feeding or pet stores. You can make your own with eggshells. Sterilize them first by heating them in an oven for at placing water in a dish, providing a pedestal birdbath, or creating a recirculating fountain or even a pond.

Birdbaths are pretty easy to add to your yard. They can be placed on the ground, mounted on a pedestal, or hung from a tree or deck. It's a good idea to place a birdbath away from your birdfeeders or other areas where birds could perch above the bath, so bird droppings and seed hulls don't fall into the water. If you have cats in your neighborhood, place your birdbath 10 to 12 feet (3 to 3.7 m) from shrubs so the cats can't sneak up on birds at the bath. Predators such as hawks can also be a problem, and having the shrub 10 feet (3 m) away can provide shelter for the birds when they flee the birdbath.

Birdbaths come in many shapes, sizes, and materials. Decorative baths may look nice but are often hard to clean and may be too steep or deep for the birds to bathe safely. Birdbaths should have a gradual slope, and if deeper than 3 inches (7.6 cm), add some stones. Birds will bathe and drink in different depths of water, so even if your bath is less than 3 inches (7.6 cm) deep, you can still add a stone or two.

You can attach a dripper or mister to your birdbath to provide a source of moving water. Most drippers and misters are easy to install and do not require an electrical outlet. They operate from your outdoor water faucet, so be sure to place the birdbath close to the water source. If the hose that connects to a water source is along a path, you can dig a trench and bury the hose underground. You will be amazed at the action at your birdbath when you add moving water. Birds will land on the dripper spout and creep down to the end to drink water.

Try to place the birdbath in a location where it will receive no more than four

BIRD BATHS RUN THE

GAMUT FROM SIMPLE TO OPULENT. IT IS A QUESTION OF INDIVIDUAL TASTE.

WHEN PLACING A FEEDER IN YOUR BACKYARD, CHOOSE A SPOT WHERE YOU CAN EASILY OBSERVE THE BIRDS THAT EAT THERE.

considered only a quick short-term fix and could potentially harm the birds.

If water sources are frozen and you provide a bath for birds, you may find that you have regular winter visitors. Many baths can be left out year-round, though some concrete or ceramic baths may be too fragile to leave outdoors all winter. They may crack or crumble because they absorb moisture which contracts and expands in freezing temperatures. Ceramic baths should be taken indoors or covered with protective plastic to prevent moisture from reaching the bath during freezing weather. Some concrete baths can handle the winter months with an added birdbath heater. A plastic dish with a heater on the bath pedestal can be offered as an alternative to using the cement top. A bird can access the water even if some of it is frozen. As long as there is an opening in the water, the heater is doing its job.

to five hours of sun in a day. Partial shade makes algae easier to control and will keep the water temperature a little cooler; evaporation should also be a little slower. Regular cleaning of the birdbath will help reduce algae in the bath. Every few days, scrub the bath regularly with a stiff scrub brush, rinse well, and replace with fresh water. If algae or stains are a reoccurring problem, a bleach solution of ten parts water to one part bleach can be used to clean the bath. Rinse well and replace with fresh water. Do not use additives in the water. They are usually

CREATING A HABITAT

All forms of wildlife need the basics of food, water, shelter, and places to raise their young. When creating a wildlife habitat, you should take into consideration the birds you already have as visitors and the ones you wish to attract. Creating a plan for your backyard habitat will help you create one you want to enjoy and that will benefit the birds.

Take an inventory of what you already have in your yard. You may find it easier if you categorize your habitat elements. Once you have compiled a list, make a plan as to what else you may need. Even if you don't provide them all in one week, chart them in your plan so you have a clear picture of what your end result may be.

You might think bird feeders are an easy way to provide food for birds, but there's an

SUNFLOWER SEEDS ARE THE ONE FOOD THAT NEARLY ALL SEED-EATING BIRDS WILL EAT. CHICKADEES AND NUTHATCHES, FOR EXAMPLE, WILL CHOOSE A SEED FROM THE FEEDER AND FLY AWAY TO BREAK IT OPEN.

BACKYARD HABITAT TIPS

Creating a sanctuary right in your own backyard is a great way to bring birds right to you! A combination of habitat elements (food, water, shelter, and places to raise young) can ensure that you attract a variety of birds close to home. Food can include feeders filled with the right kinds of foods for the birds you want to attract, and Native plants and flowers can also supply regular food. Plants that provide nectar for birds and butterflies are colorful additions to any yard. Many native flowering plants provide nectar from the flowers and later seeds, once the flower heads produce seeds. A variety of plants can provide a regular cycle of flowers, seeds, or fruits for birds. Providing the right kinds of elements for a habitat to attract a variety of birds can bring them up close. All you have to do is look out your window or step out your door.

easier way. Even seed-eating birds supplement their diet with insects as well as berries. Plants native to the soils and climate of your area provide the best overall food sources for wildlife. Native plants generally require less fertilizer and water and have evolved over time to live in your area. They may support 10 to 50 times more species of native wildlife—mostly insects, which are an important food source for birds—compared to non-native plants.

Using a variety of plant species with varying flowering or fruiting times will ensure there is a year-round supply of natural food for the birds. In the spring and summer, nectar-producing plants will attract orioles and hummingbirds in addition to butterflies. Azaleas, butterfly bushes, and crabapples also produce nectar for birds. Summer-bearing shrubs include blackberry, serviceberry, mulberry, and blueberry. Fall-fruiting plants include dogwoods, mountain ash, and winterberries. The fall-fruiting plants are especially useful to migratory birds as well as the regular backyard visitors. Plants that retain their fruit during the winter include hollies, snowberries, and sumac. Plants will also attract a variety of beneficial insects for birds. While trees such as oaks, pines, hickories, and walnuts produce nuts and seeds, they take a little longer to reach maturity. Carefully selected plantings can provide cover and/or places to raise young.

Landscaping for the best wildlife habitat should include plants ranging in size and density from small evergreen shrubs to tall, full-grown trees. Birds need cover for protection from severe weather and predators. This can be provided in many forms such as log and brush piles.

The following are some quick backyard bird habitat tips.

Mulching

Mulch keeps water from evaporating and keeps the soil moist; it also helps control unwanted weeds. This can reduce how much time you spend watering your yard. Mulch eventually breaks down and can provide nutrients to the soil.

Reducing Lawn

Lawns often require a lot of work to keep up. Because lawns are only comprised of a few types of plants, they do not provide much value for wildlife. The more diverse the plants, the better for birds. If you do have a manicured lawn, reduce or eliminate the fertilizers and chemicals you use on your yard. Keep your lawn mowed at 3 inches (7.2 cm) to help combat weeds.

Providing Birdhouses and Nest Boxes

By providing nest boxes you can encourage birds to raise their young in your backyard habitat. Birds are fascinating to watch, and you can enjoy the courtship and rearing of the young right in your own backyard! Some birds have been known to pick material off clothes hanging on a clothesline, or come right into an open window to fetch materials for their nests.

Some birds nest in cavities, using birdhouses or natural holes in trees to nest; many others build nests on ledges or roofs, in bushes, trees, or hanging baskets; still others nest on the ground. Some birds—cardinals, doves, and orioles, for example—are not cavity-nesters, and they build their nests in vines, bushes, and trees. Wrens, swallows, bluebirds, purple martins, chickadees, and titmice are some of the species that readily use nest boxes.

If you want to put up a nest box, make sure that it is well-constructed, durable, and clean. It should also be made with the birds in mind, and easy for you to monitor.

WATCHING THE BEHAVIOR OF NESTING BIRDS REARING THEIR YOUNG IS EXCITING FOR ALL LEVELS OF ENTHUSIASTS.

PROVIDING SHELTER AND PLACES TO RAISE YOUNG

Watching birds in courtship and watching them create their nests and raise their young can be a fascinating experience. Being able to provide the elements necessary for the birds can help you experience these wonderful events. Being able to provide the right shelter for the needs of the birds in your habitat is important.

Shelter can include bushes and trees for birds to nest in as well as birdhouses. The types of birds you see in your habitat will help you determine the types of houses you can provide. Not all birds use houses, and there are some birds you may not want to invite into the houses you place in your backyard sanctuary.

TOP LEFT: RELATED TO THE CHICKADEE, THE TUFTED TITMOUSE READILY COMES TO BIRD FEEDERS. TOP RIGHT: THE GILA WOODPECKER IS A NOISY AND BOLD DENIZEN OF THE SOUTHWEST DESERT REGIONS, NESTING IN SAGUARO CACTI. BOTTOM RIGHT: THE HOUSE WREN IS VERY ACTIVE AND INQUISITIVE; THEY CAN SCOLD YOU IF COME TOO NEAR THEIR NEST. BOTTOM LEFT: BLACK-CHINNED HUMMINGBIRDS ARE REGULAR VISITORS TO GARDENS AND WILL OFTEN NEST IN BACKYARDS.

Features of a Good Nest Box:

- Untreated wood
- Walls ¾ inch (1.9 cm) thick
- Sloped roof, extended over entrance hole
- Rough or grooved interior walls
- Drainage holes in the floor
- Ventilation holes in upper walls
- Access for easy monitoring and cleaning
- No outside perches

The height of the nest box depends on the species. For most backyard cavity nesters, a height of at least 5 feet (1.5 m) is recommended. Don't put birdhouses near bird feeders. Birds feeding too close to a birdhouse can create unnecessary stress on nestlings. The easiest way to discourage predatory cats, snakes, raccoons, and chipmunks is to mount the house on a metal pole or use a metal predator guard on a wood post. These are less vulnerable than houses nailed to tree trunks or hung from tree limbs.

Birdhouse Birds

Over two dozen North American birds will nest in birdhouses. Look at the list below and see which birds are in your neighborhood.

Chickadees, Nuthatches, and Titmice

If you put a properly designed nest box in a semi-wooded or wooded yard, you may attract chickadees, titmice, and nuthatches, who all have similar eating habits. Put chickadee houses at eye-level, hanging them from limbs. The entrance hole should be 1 inch (2.5 cm) to attract chickadees yet exclude the English house sparrow, which can kill baby birds and take over their nests.

Bluebirds

If you live near an old farm field, orchard, cemetery, or golf course, you may have a good chance of attracting bluebirds. They prefer nest boxes on a post between 4 and 5 feet (1.2–1.5 cm) high. Bluebirds will also use abandoned woodpecker nest holes. An

USUALLY FOUND IN SMALL FLOCKS, THE WESTERN BLUEBIRD'S SONG IS NOT CONSIDERED AS SWEET AS ITS EASTERN COUSIN'S.

opening about 1½ inches (3.8 cm) wide is large enough for bluebirds, but small enough to deter starlings. Starlings and house sparrows have been known to kill baby bluebirds, as well as adults sitting on the nest.

Robins

Robins build their nests in crotches of trees or bushes. A nesting platform can be offered for robins if your habitat doesn't have suitable trees or bushes. Pick a spot 6 feet (1.8 m) or higher up under the overhang of a shed or porch.

Wrens

House wrens will nest practically anywhere, be it potted plants, old tin cans, or nest boxes. Try nest boxes with a 1 by 2 inch (2.5 by 5 cm) hole. For Carolina wrens, a larger bird than the house wren, use a box with a 1½ to 2½ inch (3.8-6.4 cm) opening. Wrens are notorious for filling up a cavity with twigs. Male house wrens will often build several nests for a female to choose from, so hang several boxes. Wrens are sociable and will accept nest boxes quite close to your house.

THE GRACKLE IS COMMON IN MANY AREAS, INCLUDING FARMLANDS, TOWNS, GROVES, AND BACKYARDS. WHEN COURTING, IT WILL FLUFF OUT ITS FEATHERS WHILE SPREADING ITS WINGS AND TAIL FEATHERS.

WHILE THERE ARE MANY DECORATIVE BIRDHOUSES AVAILABLE TODAY, IT IS BEST TO CHOOSE ONE THAT IS SURE TO PROVIDE A SAFE AND SECURE PLACE FOR BIRDS TO NEST.

Tree and Violet-Green Swallows
The ideal setting for swallows is on the edge of a field near a lake or pond. Tree swallows will nest in bluebird boxes on poles. Space the boxes about 7 to 10 feet (2.1 to 3 m) apart. Violet-green swallows nest in forested mountains of the west, and boxes placed on poles in a semi-open woodland should attract them.

Purple Martins
While many people believe that purple martins eat a lot of mosquitoes, they really prefer dragonflies, insects which prey on mosquito larvae. Your chances of attracting martins is best if you put a house on the edge of a pond or river, surrounded by a field or lawn where the birds can feed on insects. Martins are colonial nesters; they nest in groups so you'll need a house with at least four nesting rooms with a 2¼ inches (5.7 cm) entrance hole about 1½ inches (3.8 cm) above the floor for each compartment. Gourds may also be made into houses by making an entrance hole and providing drainage. Railings and perches are not necessary on gourds.

PLANTING A VARIETY OF NATIVE PLANTS IN YOUR YARD WILL ATTRACT A VARIETY OF BIRDS.

PROTECTING YOUR BACKYARD BIRDS

The thrill of being able to watch birds up close is worth the extra effort of creating the right environment to satisfy their needs. Unfortunately, in addition to the challenges they face outside the boundaries of your yard, there are some dangers that backyard birds face. You can make your yard a safe place for the birds that visit your habitat.

Properly placed and supplied feeders and baths are an asset to any yard. Unfor-

A BALTIMORE ORIOLE NEST NEAR A FISHING AREA CONTAINS POTENTIALLY DANGEROUS
FISHING LINE AND HOOK. EFFORTS SHOULD BE MADE TO MINIMIZE THESE RISKS.

TODAY, MANY WINDOWS CAN BE DESIGNED TO HELP PREVENT BIRDS FROM FLYING INTO THEM.

tunately, they can be sources of diseases that can kill or harm birds. Some diseases that can be spread include mycoplasmal conjunctivitis, aspergillosis, avian chlamydia, and trichomoniasis. Providing clean feeders and birdbaths can help eliminate many of these dangers. Discouraging large concentrations of birds and maintaining feeders and baths will also control the spread of disease.

Some backyard birds are eaten by other wildlife, including raptors. Hawks are natural predators; however, you can provide safe places for birds to flee by placing feeders about 10 feet (3 m) from dense vegetation, brush piles, or even a rock wall. Cats are another predator and can use the cover to lie in wait for unsuspecting prey.

Scientists estimate that free-roaming cats kill hundreds of millions of birds, small mammals, reptiles, and amphibians each year. There are more than 90 million pet cats in the United States, and many of these are allowed outside on a regular basis. In addition, there are millions of stray and feral cats. Cat predation is an added stress to birds and other wildlife already struggling to survive human impacts such as habitat loss, pollution, and pesticides. The American Bird Conservancy (ABC) launched the Cats Indoors! Campaign to educate cat owners, policymakers, and the general public about the damage that cats can do to birds and other wildlife. Cats kept indoors are healthier and safer, and the birds and wildlife will benefit, too.

I will never forget the first time I saw my indoor/outdoor cat catch an American goldfinch off the feeder outside my kitchen window. I was stunned and mortified. I realized that my cat was catching birds almost every day, and while the first few weeks of keeping her inside were hard, I knew she wasn't killing birds anymore. I also knew that she wasn't in danger of getting hit by a car, getting lost, or contracting a disease.

WATCH OUT FOR WINDOWS

Clear and reflective window panes in homes or commercial buildings are a passive killer of wild birds worldwide. Birds do not recognize glass as an object they cannot fly through. The reflections in the window seen by the birds appear to be just another flight path, and fatal or injurious collisions are inevitable. There are many solutions that effectively reduce or eliminate bird strikes. Protective measures range from physical barriers that keep birds from striking it, to making a window more visible. Taking one or more of the following measures, especially during spring and fall migration, will help reduce injuries caused by home and office windows:

- Place bird feeders more than 30 feet (9.1 m) from the glass surface to eliminate the hazard for feeding birds.
- Place vertical exterior tape strips not more than 4 inches (10 cm) apart on windows. They are a better deterrent than decals with cut-outs of raptors or leaded glass decorations, which are only moderately successful.
- Keep interior vertical blinds with the slats half open or close drapes and turn interior lights off to reduce the effect of a see-through passage behind the glass.
- Soap windows to make them opaque. This is not very pretty but effective.
- Plant shade trees no less than 3 feet (0.9 m) from the window to cut down on some of the reflection.
- Use window screens.
- Cover the surface with objects less than 4 inches (10 cm) apart—anything that makes glass more visible will suffice.

ORPHAN BIRDS

Many backyards attract nesting birds and therefore often have baby birds. When most baby birds hatch, they are dependent on their parents to feed them and keep them safe. As the babies grow and then fledge—leave the nest—they will stay close to their parents, watching and learning how to forage for food. It is at this time many people think the baby birds are orphaned and may need help.

In most cases, if you find a baby bird, leave it alone. If the bird has feathers, it may be a fledged bird, and a parent bird is probably close by. As long as the bird is in no danger from cats or other predators, it is best to watch it from a distance. View for two hours before determining that the bird needs human help. If the bird appears as though it has fallen from a nest, an attempt to locate the nest can be made, and the bird can be carefully returned.

Birds do not have a true sense of smell, so it is a myth that birds will reject a baby bird if touched by a human. A baby bird that has been touched by a human, however, does make it easier for a predator to locate. If you find a bird that you have determined is truly orphaned, it is best to call a rehabilitator to care for the bird. For all but a few birds, possessing one requires a special permit and training. The care of injured birds and wildlife should be left to people who know how to do it. Sometimes you can find a rehabilitator through your local veterinarian, or you can check www.wildliferehabber.org.

CHAPTER FOUR

BIRDING ON LOCATION
TAKING YOUR HOBBY ON THE ROAD

- *Places to find birds*

- *Birding hot spots*

- *Birding by habitat*

- *Birding from a vehicle*

- *Birding in a group*

There are many places to find birds, some of which may surprise you. I keep a notebook to record the birds I see. Rather than a life list, which tracks the number of different species observed, it is more of a travel log of what I find and where. It is helpful when I plan a return trip, and lets me apply this knowledge to areas where I plan to bird next. If I know I have seen a bird in a certain area, I can look for it in a similar habitat.

Recording the birds and places is also helpful when people ask what I have seen and where. Other birders enjoy it when you share this information because it makes it easier for them when they visit an area. They increase their chances of finding the birds they want to see by targeting a specific location. Birders who use listserves regularly do this.

PLACES TO FIND BIRDS

Some of the best places to find birds include parks, nature centers, and national refuges. All of these places usually have well-established trail systems and areas known for finding birds. They are generally open to the public.

Most birding guides will list the places you are most likely to find birds. Throughout North America there are at least a dozen top hot spots every birdwatcher would recommend and another few hundred highly regarded spots. A quick search on the Internet can yield a list. Most birders have their own list of not-to-be-missed spots and personal favorites.

BIRDING HOT SPOTS
The "Ding" Darling National Wildlife Refuge, Sanibel Island, Florida
A must-visit spot, especially if you would like to see a roseate spoonbill or a white pelican. The refuge offers a variety of walking trails, and, for the person who likes to bird from the car, the drive provides excellent views of many birds. Be sure to visit when the tide is low,

HOT SPOTS ARE PLACES WITH AN UNUSUALLY HIGH CONCENTRATION OF BIRDS.

WHERE THE BIRDS ARE

You can find birds almost any place you go. The next time you are at a shopping center on a summer evening, listen for the distinctive *beent* of the common nighthawks as they circle for insects above the parking lot lights. Another place I enjoy is the baseball field at night. The lights attract a huge number of insects, and the birds and bats congregate to feast on them. Once you start noticing birds and thinking about what habitats are associated with them, you will broaden your birding horizons.

because you will see many shorebirds. A quick stop at the visitor center will help you figure out which trails to take and what birds have been seen lately. (www.fws.gov/dingdarling)

Babcock-Cecil M. Webb Wildlife Management Area, Florida

At more than 79,000 acres (32,000ha), this unique area is the seventh largest wildlife management area in Florida and part of the Great Florida Birding Trail system. It is among the last undeveloped expanses of wet pine flatwoods in southwest Florida and features freshwater marshes, seasonal ponds, hardwood hammocks, and prairies. Special birding opportunities include brown-headed nuthatches, American and least bitterns, sandhill cranes, Bachman's sparrow, the rare red-cockaded woodpecker, and more.

The Audubon Corkscrew Swamp Sanctuary, Florida

One of my favorite places to birdwatch. Located an hour or so from Naples, it is a great place to see many wading and waterbirds, warblers, hawks, and eagles. The wood storks, however, are a highlight of the trip. If you plan to see the storks, your visit needs to be timed properly to catch them on their nests. Some years are good for the storks and others are not. Water and food levels must be adequate when the adults begin to arrive in late December and January. If the water is too high or too low, it alters the availability of food for the storks and their young. The chicks must fledge before the rainy season begins, when the water level becomes too high. If it is a bad

PLACING NEST BOXES IN YOUR BACKYARD HABITAT WILL PROVIDE A SAFE HOME FOR CAVITY NESTING BIRDS.

year for storks, there are still plenty of great opportunities to birdwatch. The self-guiding boardwalk has signs to help you and, on busy days, volunteers are often situated along the walk to help you see nesting owls or other

HAWK MOUNTAIN SANCTUARY OFFERS AN OPPORTUNITY TO SEE THE MIGRATION OF A VARIETY OF RAPTORS. AN OWL DECOY IS PERCHED OVER THE NORTH LOOKOUT.

wildlife sights. This is a great spot to take your family. They have a nature center with loaner binoculars and field guides. (www.audubon.org/local/sanctuary/corkscrew)

Point Pelee National Park, Ontario, Canada

This is a terrific spot during spring migration. The bird list includes 372 species. During spring migration it looks like warblers are raining from the sky. Exhausted birds will fly the 6 to 8 miles (30-40 km) across Lake Erie and land on the point before continuing their migration farther north. If you enjoy butterflies, visit in the fall during monarch butterfly migration. (www.pc.gc.ca/pn-np/on/pelee)

Ramsey Canyon, Arizona

This is the place if you are looking for hummingbirds. The canyon boasts up to 14 species of hummingbirds, as well as painted redstarts.

The best months for birding at the preserve are April through September. Spring weather is unpredictable, though it is usually dry and cool at night. August is peak hummingbird season. Keep an eye out for mountain lions as well as other great wildlife. (www.nature.org/wherewework/northamerica/states/arizona/preserves/art1973.html)

After you bird in Ramsey Canyon, be sure to stop in the Sonora Desert Museum to bird the habitat around the property. You will be sure to find cactus wren, gila woodpecker, Gambel's quail, and the greater roadrunner. (www.desertmuseum.org)

Cape May Bird Observatory, New Jersey

Known for its vast concentrations of autumn migrants, Cape May has recorded over 400 species of birds. Nearly a million shorebirds gather along the beaches of

Delaware Bay each spring including loons, gannets, cormorants, and other seabirds that migrate within sight of land. Cape May is also a great spot for birds of prey, which are tallied at an official hawk watch every autumn. (www.njaudubon.org)

Hawk Mountain Sanctuary, Pennsylvania

Another fall hot spot for hawk watching is Hawk Mountain Sanctuary, located along the Appalachian Flyway in east–central Pennsylvania. The mountaintop vista and many hiking trails are worth seeing at almost any time of year, but the highlight is the fall hawk migration. This opportunity is the best in the northeast. Between mid-August and mid-December an average of 20,000 hawks, eagles, and falcons pass through the Sanctuary's North Lookout. Information about the numbers of hawks is available

THE AMERICAN BITTERN IS A SOLITARY HERON AND STALKS QUIETLY THROUGH MARSHES AND REEDS IN SHALLOW WATER. IT EATS SNAKES, FISH, FROGS, AND AQUATIC INSECTS.

GETTING TO KNOW YOU

Some birds have highly-specialized habitat needs and don't venture far from their special niche. Such specific needs are almost always associated with gathering food. Many birds may occupy the same habitat, but how and what food they gather may differ. Knowing birds' characteristics can help you guess where you might find them or, if you are in a specific habitat, you can guess what kinds of birds you may find there.

on their website. Time your visit to occur during peak migration in September and November. (www.hawkmountain.org)

Santa Ana National Wildlife Refuge, Texas

This birder's delight is located in the lower Rio Grande Valley of the southernmost part of Texas. The 397 species of birds found there include black-bellied and fulvous whistling-ducks, cinnamon teal, white ibis, and long-billed dowitcher.

Migrating raptors that fly over the refuge in spring and fall may include the rare hook-billed kite and gray hawk. Other specialties found in the valley include the buff-bellied hummingbird, roseate spoonbill, plain chachalaca, red-billed pigeon, and ringed and green kingfishers, among many

THE SANTA ANA NATIONAL WILDLIFE REFUGE IN TEXAS HAS MANY BIRDS THAT ARE UNIQUE TO THAT AREA.

others. The great kiskadee and green jay are a loud reminder of the tropical nature of the area. (www.fws.gov/refuges/profiles/index. cfm?id=21551)

Point Reyes National Seashore, California

Encompassing more than 70,000 acres (28,000 ha) of habitat harbor with nearly 490 avian species, Point Reyes' coastal location offers a wealth of unspoiled habitats; it has estuaries, grasslands, coastal scrub, and forest that attract many migrating and wintering birds. The projection of the peninsula into the sea makes Point Reyes National Seashore a landing spot for many migrants, as well as some unexpected visitors from time to time. The entire family can enjoy this spot because the wildlife is abundant, and it is also a great place to go whale watching. (www.nps.gov/pore)

Bosque del Apache National Wildlife Refuge, New Mexico

A wintering home for sandhill cranes, the refuge will host as many as 14,000 between November and the end of February. Watching the cranes fly into the refuge is a spectacular sight and one every birdwatcher should experience. Tens of thousands of geese and ducks gather here each autumn and stay through the winter. Northern Indiana also hosts a great spot for watching the gathering of sandhill cranes at Jasper–Pulaski Fish and Wildlife Area in Medaryville, Indiana. (http://www.fws. gov/southwest/refuges/newmex/bosque)

Each state and province has their own places for terrific birdwatching. Most birdwatchers

will seek out areas where they can find higher concentrations of birds or that have rare or unique species. Keep track of the places you visit and what birds you see.

BIRDING BY HABITAT

Birds live in habitats that provide food, water, shelter, and a safe place to raise their families. While many birds share similar habitats, there are specific habitats where you will only find certain types of birds. Learning about the bird's requirements will help you locate more of them.

Habitat types include: coastal shores, open oceans, forests, grasslands, rivers, lakes, ponds, marshes, and swamps. Birds that live in these habitats have adapted to survive in them. It is not impossible to find a bird outside of the habitat most suited for it, but it is more likely that you will find birds in their preferred areas.

Coastal Shores

Coastal shores include sandy beaches, rocky shores, coastal wetlands, bays, and estuaries. The habitat of these shores differs depending on their geographic location and how the environments relate to the water source. Estuaries, a salt and freshwater combination, are important habitats for birds because they provide a resting place for shorebirds during migration as well as places to feed and to breed. Many types of waterfowl rely on estuaries year-round.

Species of birds such as dunlin sandpipers feed in the muddy shores of bays. Tides rise and fall in the bays forming mudflats that are exposed at low tide, and which allow dunlins to probe the muddy soils with their long bills. In the winter season and during migration, the bays and estuaries attract a wide variety of shorebirds. Birds such as the long-billed curlew probe deep into the sand for marine worms and mollusks that other shorebirds cannot reach. Bays and estuaries are excellent places for birding all year-round.

Beaches provide a vital habitat for birds. You will find terns, gulls, plovers, and sandpipers there. Black skimmers and common terns can be seen skimming along the water in search of food. Great blue herons and green herons are found stalking their prey along the water's edge. Least sandpipers, semipalmated plovers, and ruddy turnstones are often seen feeding on shores of the Atlantic coast.

Beaches can be especially important during the spring and fall migration because they provide feeding areas for many species of shorebirds. One of the most important areas in eastern North America is Delaware Bay, where plovers, sandpipers, and other shorebirds migrating north from South America stop and feed on the horseshoe crab eggs. The red knot, for example, travels from its wintering grounds in Chile to its breeding habitats in the arctic of Canada. It travels an estimated annual round-trip of almost 19,888 miles (32,000 km). Without this beach and food source, the birds would not survive their long journey.

Oceans

The ocean can be a great place to go birdwatching. To watch seabirds soaring over the water is an amazing sight. The most abundant birds found on the ocean are the shearwaters, petrels, and albatrosses. Seabirds drink saltwater and have special glands that filter salt from their bloodstream. Most of these birds are fish eaters who catch their food at or just below the surface of the water. These birds include the Atlantic puffin, black-legged kittiwake, black scoter, common eider, double-crested cormorant, northern gannet, and oldsquaw. Many organizations and businesses offer ocean birding trips, and it is worth investigating a guided tour.

Forests

Forests vary greatly depending on where they are. Some regions contain deciduous trees that have no leaves during winter. The most typical forest in the east is a beech–sugar maple type that extends from western New York to Indiana. In Kentucky and Tennessee, there are white basswood and yellow buckeye trees. Forests that contain a variety of different trees are called mixed deciduous.

FOUND ON NEARLY EVERY OCEAN BEACH IN THE WORLD, THE SANDERLING CAN BE SEEN DARTING INTO THE RETREATING SURF TO FEED.

THE RING TEAL IS CONSIDERED AN EXOTIC DUCK RARELY SEEN OUTSIDE OF A ZOO.

THE EASTERN TOWHEE, PART OF
THE SPARROW FAMILY, SCRATCHES
ON THE FOREST FLOOR FOR
INSECTS AND SEEDS.

Forest habitats include boreal forests that are characterized by evergreen and coniferous trees, such as species of spruce, fir, and pine. Frequently, the boreal forest includes birches, poplars, and alders. Birding in the boreal forest will reward you with sightings of goshawks, spruce grouse, gray jay, and crossbills. Unfortunately, it is often hard to bird there, because these forests are typically very dense and when it is breeding season for the birds, it is the peak season for insects. The birds love the bugs, but you may not!

Florida has mangrove forests. These offer a unique habitat for many birds. Roseate spoonbills, smooth-billed anis, and yellow-billed cuckoos will make their nests in the mangroves.

Grasslands

Grasslands are large terrains of grasses and flowers. Latitude, soil, and climate determine what types of plants grow in particular grasslands. These plants typically grow from the bottom instead of the top, and their stems can grow back after being burned off in a fire. There are grassland birds almost everywhere in North America. In the east, eastern meadowlarks, ring-necked pheasants, bobolinks, red-winged blackbirds, and many types of sparrows are attracted to grassland and agricultural fields. Owls and hawks can be seen hunting for food over these fields. Short-eared owls and northern harriers nest on the ground in grasslands. Many grassland areas are threatened due to suburban development and agricultural use. However, some farming does benefit birds.

In the Great Lakes, forests are known as the hemlock hardwoods, where hemlock, beech, and sugar maple trees are common. West of Illinois the forest starts to contain a large number of oak trees. The types of trees that are present often determine which birds use that forest. The deciduous woods are homes to many smaller birds such as the migrating warblers in the east and the tanagers in the south. Some other birds you may find in forests include: Acadian flycatcher, American redstart, American woodcock, black-and-white warbler, black-billed cuckoo, cedar waxwing, Cooper's hawk, eastern wood-pewee, rose-breasted grosbeak, scarlet tanager, sharp-shinned hawk, and the pileated woodpecker.

TOP: BLACK VULTURES FEED MOSTLY ON DEAD ANIMALS, WHICH THEY FIND BY SIGHT AND SMELL. UNLIKE MOST OTHER BIRDS, VULTURES HAVE A KEEN SENSE OF SMELL. BOTTOM RIGHT: THE GRAY JAY IS WELL KNOWN FOR ITS HABIT OF STORING FOOD FOR THE WINTER AND STEALING FROM PICNICS AND CAMPSITES. BOTTOM LEFT: GRASSLANDS PROVIDE AMPLE HABITATS INCLUDING SEEDS, INSECTS, AND NESTING AREAS.

Barn swallows are the most common birds on farmlands and will often nest in the rafters and eaves of the barns. Barn owls will also utilize farm buildings, but many barns are more modern in design and don't allow for birds to nest freely in them. Barn owls can be very beneficial as they prey on mice, rats, and voles that can damage crops. Vegetation that often grows along the fences and fields on farms attracts pheasants, meadowlarks, catbirds, sparrows, and waxwings.

Rivers and Streams

Rivers and streams are bodies of water that move constantly. Streams usually feed into the rivers. There are rapidly-moving streams, found in mountainous areas, and slower-moving streams which have a slight gradient. Most streams have slippery rocks that are

DRIVING TRAILS ALLOW YOU TO BE LESS NOTICEABLE WHILE BIRDWATCHING.

STAY IN YOUR CAR

There are a variety of birding places that have driving trails. It may seem not quite like a way to watch birds, but there are advantages to staying in your car. "Ding" Darling National Wildlife Refuge has a great driving trail which allows you to drive slowly and stop when you see the birds you want to watch. You can get out of your car to take a picture or set up your scope to take a longer look at the birds. Another benefit to staying in your air-conditioned car is that you can avoid the bugs and weather.

coated with algae. Rivers and streams are often lined with mature trees, grasses, bushes, and wildflowers. Along wooded riverbanks you can find northern orioles, warblers, vireos, and wrens. Also look for kingfishers along the banks of rivers and streams.

Lake and Ponds

Ponds are characteristically small and shallow, whereas lakes are deeper and larger bodies of water. Ponds and shallow lakes provide algae which feeds ducks, geese, and swans. Along the shores, plants such as cattails and bulrushes provide great nesting habitat. Keep an eye out for American coot, bald eagle, belted kingfisher, blue-winged teal, canvasback duck, common goldeneye, common merganser, and yellow-crowned night heron. Urban ponds and lakes often provide great habitat for geese and ducks, especially the Canada goose and the mallard duck.

Marshes and Swamps

The water level in a marsh can be shallow or deep. It is filled with reeds, rushes, and cattails and is usually open with no trees. Marshes can be found along streams in poorly-drained areas and also develop in the shallower water along the borders of lakes, ponds, and rivers. A swamp is either completely or partially wooded with trees and shrubs. Swamp soils are a dark mucky color and have some standing water. A wide variety of birds such as the American bittern, common yellowthroat, gadwall, limpkin, red-winged blackbird, and sora rails can be found in marshes and swamps.

WATER ALWAYS SIGNALS AN OPPORTUNITY TO SEE A VARIETY OF BIRDS.

Field and bird finding guides usually list a bird's preferred habitats. The books and guides also provide maps to indicate what time of year the bird is likely to be seen. Don't forget to consider the migration of the birds. There are some habitats that serve simply as a stopover point for birds on their migratory journey. Other habitats serve as breeding and nesting areas and may be used by birds only during their breeding season.

BIRDING FROM A VEHICLE

There are a number of spots where you can bird from your car, bike, or wheelchair. If you are traveling with an older or a very young family member, birding in your car can allow you to birdwatch even if family members may not be able to walk a trail. If you travel with a pet—we often take our collie dog, Chico, with

THE POPULAR RED-WINGED BLACKBIRD IS A COMMON SIGHT IN MARSHY FIELDS, SWAMPS, AND HAYFIELDS. THEY ARE BOLD AND WILL CHASE LARGER BIRDS IF THREATENED.

us—you will find birding from your car very dog-friendly. Check the rules at the places you visit to make sure they are okay with your dog being on the property. I have included some of the friendliest places for various types of vehicle birdwatching. Check with each location to be sure they can meet your needs.

Many of the hot spots for birding also have areas where you can easily drive your car. In many places, special accommodations can be made if you call ahead and ask how to get close to a walkway or viewing platform. Many refuges and nature centers have loaner wheelchairs or golf carts to make birding trails more accessible. It is frustrating to plan a trip only to find out you can't get to where you want to go, or access to bikes or watercraft is prohibited. Call ahead to avoid disappointment.

Bikes are not the easiest way to bird, but it may make the trip more enjoyable for other family members. The birdwatcher in the group can fall behind to watch a bird and then cycle fast to catch up. Remember that the movement and noise of a bike may interfere with any birdwatching activity.

Birdwatching while kayaking or canoeing is one of my family's favorite activities. Being in the kayak allows us to get quite close to the aquatic plants and birds. We can float downstream and, if we are quiet, we can sneak up to many waterbirds. Many places rent kayaks and canoes or will allow access if you bring your own. Call ahead to check their rules, including any safety requirements such as lifejackets, throw ropes, emergency gear, and the like.

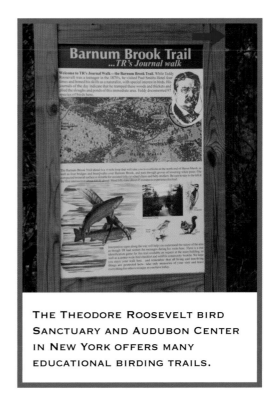

THE THEODORE ROOSEVELT BIRD SANCTUARY AND AUDUBON CENTER IN NEW YORK OFFERS MANY EDUCATIONAL BIRDING TRAILS.

"Ding" Darling National Wildlife Refuge is one of the easiest birding places to bird by car. In fact, it is visited mostly by cars. Occasionally, you can find bikes on the drive, and sometimes tour companies will take their canoeing or kayaking customers there so people can explore the water areas.

The dirt trails and beaches of Point Reyes National Seashore are accessible by an all-terrain wheelchair, but you need to have a person with you who is able to help with the wheelchair. Check with the park for a list of wheelchair-accessible trails and the availability of wheelchairs.

Gray's Harbor National Wildlife Refuge near Olympia, Washington has wheelchair-accessible trails; however they do not allow pets, boats, or any kind of bicycles.

Muir Woods National Monument in California offers good wheelchair-accessible trails for forest birdwatching. Being able to walk or wheel a chair through the magnificent redwood trees that tower above you is quite breathtaking. Go deeper into the woods to enjoy the birds and avoid the tourist trails. (Many of the deeper trails are wheelchair accessible as well.)

Everglades National Park in Florida has many touring options. It has a boardwalk on the Anhinga Trail at the north end of the park that winds through marshland habitat, where you can get a good look at many waterbirds. The park also has other handicapped-accessible trails that are wheelchair-friendly. Some trails are accessible to bikes, and some areas are dog-friendly. It is also easy to drive through the park.

Corkscrew Swamp Sanctuary (near Naples, Florida) allows wheelchairs on their self-guiding boardwalk. They also have a limited number of wheelchairs to loan to visitors. However, bikes and dogs are not permitted.

Cape May in Delaware Bay is the place to watch hawk migration, and the platform from where many raptors can be viewed has a wheelchair-accessible ramp.

The Santa Ana National Wildlife Refuge in Alamo, Texas has a concrete half-mile loop trail that is easy for wheelchair users, though other trails can also be accessed. There are two observation decks at Willow Lake that are also easy to use.

BIRDING IN A GROUP

Joining fellow birdwatchers on a outing has many advantages. It can be through a local nature center or bird club, an organized tour with a company that specializes in birdwatching, or a group of friends. The biggest advantage is that you usually have a trip leader who knows what birds you will see and where you are mostly likely to find them.

When you are deciding whether or not you want to go with a group, ask yourself why you want to take the trip, and do you want to see local, rare, or unusual birds? Do you want an adventure or a simple trip? Determining why you want to go and what you want to see will help you decide if you need to go with a group. There are some places off-the-beaten path that official guides know well, and they can easily find the birds in that area. Being a part of a guided trip can often ensure you will see the birds you want to find.

If you are planning a local field trip, then going with your area bird club or with the local nature center is probably best. These usually cost the price of admission into the center or park or the cost of sharing gas. If you don't know the area for the planned trip or you haven't traveled with this group before, you probably want to ask some simple questions. Will there be drinkable water available? Are there bathroom facilities? Will the group stop for lunch or should you bring your own snack? What time will the group leave and what time will it return?

If you participate in an overnight trip to a neighboring state or province, you will need to plan ahead. Most bird clubs or nature centers that plan overnight trips have a driver or share driving. Some of the travel time is at night or early in the day so you

THE POPULAR EASTERN BLUE JAY IS KNOWN FOR ITS
NOISY CHATTER, AND CAN IMITATE THE CALL OF A
RED-SHOULDERED HAWK.

restaurants, which can be expensive. Other tour companies make an effort to involve local guides and boost the economy by staying at local hotels or lodges. Additionally, some tour companies give a small percentage of their proceeds to local conservation groups.

When you choose a tour company don't be afraid to ask a lot of questions. Ask if they take care of all travel arrangements. Will you need a passport or other travel documents? Are there any medical considerations for which you need to plan? Will they donate money to the local conservation group? Do they work with Birder's Exchange to take donated equipment to the area? Ask your local bird club and other birdwatchers about trips they may have taken. It is important that you feel comfortable about taking a trip with any tour company. The American Birding Association has an ABA–endorsed tours list on their website (www.americanbirding.org/tours/index.html) and the information provided may help you get started.

Birding in a group can be great fun, but do some homework so you are prepared. Explore your options and you may discover some of the places you have only dreamed about. In most cases you will not regret birding with others and my guess is that you will want to join a group again.

don't miss valuable time in the field. Understand clearly the logistics for the trip. Is there a hotel stay involved? Are meals eaten at restaurants? What should be brought with you? What is the final cost of the trip and how much money should you have for the extras? Consider who you are traveling with and be prepared to share a ride with a variety of personalities. Being in a car or van for hours with someone you don't know well may be a great opportunity to get to know someone new, or it could be a nightmare.

Tour companies that specialize in locations known for specific birds (such as the toucan, the groove-billed ani, or the spatula-tailed hummingbird) are numerous. They vary in price depending on the location and travel requirements for the trip. Some commercial companies try to make as much money as possible. Some only employ their own guides and stay at major hotels and eat only at major

PART II

GETTING THE MOST

OUT OF BIRDING

CHAPTER FIVE

IDENTIFYING THE BIRDS
IS THAT A WARBLER OR A WIGEON? LEARNING HOW TO TELL THE DIFFERENCE

- *Birds we all know*

- *Understanding general and specific characteristics*

- *Developing your observation skills*

- *Why bird behavior matters*

- *Starting a birding journal*

Whether you are a bird-watcher or not, you can probably recognize at least ten birds. Most people can easily identify an American robin, a crow, and an English house sparrow. Additionally, most people can recognize a blue jay, a Canada goose, a rock dove (pigeon), a grackle, a European starling, a mourning dove, and a mallard duck. These birds are common in many of the places we frequent.

BIRDS WE ALL KNOW

The ten birds you can identify without a field guide may be the ten birds I mentioned, or they may be other birds you have come to know in your everyday walks around your neighborhood, shopping center, or local park. You can use these ten birds to build a foundation for learning to identify more birds as you develop your birdwatching skills.

If you can remember the basic size, color, and some behavior of those ten birds you can use this knowledge. For example, birders often start their identification process by comparing the size of the bird they are watching. Is the bird smaller or larger than a sparrow? Is it smaller than a robin or is it the size of a crow? If you determine that a bird is larger than a sparrow and about the size of a robin, you can begin to eliminate birds.

After you determine the size, look at the color and shape of the bird, as well as its bill and its feet. Often the color of the bird is a giveaway for what it may be. If a blue jay is on your list of ten birds you can recognize without a field guide, consider other blue-colored birds that you may come

RED-HEADED WOODPECKERS HAVE A STRIKING RED HEAD WITH A BLACK AND WHITE BODY. THEY ARE DECLINING DUE TO A LACK OF DEAD TREES FOR NESTING AS WELL AS NEST SITE COMPETITION WITH THE NON-NATIVE STARLING.

THE FAMILY TREE

Families of birds are broadly related and often look and act alike, which can help you identify them. Once you begin to become familiar with the characteristics of these groups, you will probably be able to make a good guess identifying a bird that is unfamiliar to you. For example, after you learn the appearance and behavior of woodpeckers, you will be able to identify the difference between woodpeckers and other birds. Woodpeckers clasp the trunk of a tree with powerful clawed feet. They lean back and support some of their weight with their stiff tail feathers. When you see a bird behaving this way, you can guess that it behaves like a woodpecker and, through a process of elimination, you can probably figure out which woodpecker it is.

UNDERSTANDING THE CHARACTERISTICS OF BIRDS CAN HELP YOU LEARN TO IDENTIFY THEM MORE READILY.

across. Bluebirds—eastern, western, or mountain—are blue, as are indigo buntings. Being able to compare their size will eliminate what the blue bird may or may not be. For example, a blue jay is the size of a robin but smaller than a crow. A bluebird is larger than a sparrow, but smaller than a robin; the indigo bunting is the size of a sparrow.

You probably can recognize more than ten birds without a field guide, though you may not know the exact name of all of them. For these, start by comparing them to the birds you know and see what characteristics the birds have in common. If you can think about these characteristics

in conjunction with your field guide, you are well on your way to creating a great list of birds you can name.

UNDERSTANDING GENERAL AND SPECIFIC CHARACTERISTICS

The different characteristics of a bird's body parts serve basic functions. These different characteristics and functions can help you identify the group of birds which will help you narrow down the identification of the bird. Some characteristics are very specific to a certain bird, which narrows the possibilities even further.

THE GOLDEN EAGLE IS A MAJESTIC HUNTER EATING MAINLY SMALL MAMMALS. WHILE ITS POPULATIONS ARE THOUGHT NOW TO BE STABLE, IT HAS DECLINED DUE TO LOSS OF HABITAT.

Generally, physical characteristics that are shared by groups of birds are easy to remember when you think of the habitats and food source of the bird. Look at the tails. Long and narrow tails are good for quick maneuvering between trees and other obstacles. Short and wide tails are used by birds that flap a lot when they fly. Fanlike tails give lift, and small tails often belong to aquatic birds.

Next, consider the feet. Webbed feet are used by swimming birds. Strong and sharp talons on raptors can grasp small prey. Tough and muscular feet belong to birds that run on the ground. Perching birds have feet designed for sitting on trees or other objects. Wings have clear purposes too. Tapered wings are good for flight. Rounded, broad wings give lift and maneuver well in tight places. Large and wide wings are good for soaring and long, narrow wings are used for gliding. Bills are also very important for bird identification. Flat and wide bills scoop food; hooked bills tear flesh; tiny, pointed bills usually belong to insect-eaters; and thick bills are good for cracking open seed.

Consider the bird's characteristics with its size, color, and habitat, and you will probably identify it easily. The following groups are just a sample of some of the characteristics groups of birds share. Apply them to groups of birds not listed below.

Herons, Egrets, Ibises, Storks

- Long-legged and wade in water
- Long-necked
- Bill size and shape depends on how the bird fishes

Eagles, Hawks, Falcons

- Short, hooked bills
- Sharp, grasping talons
- Strong fliers
- Females are usually larger than male

Kingfishers

- Found mostly along banks of water
- Stout body and short neck
- Crested head
- Short and rounded wings

Woodpeckers

- Strong bill for drilling into wood for food and excavating nest cavities
- Pointed, stiff tail feathers to prop up their bodies on trees
- Undulated flight pattern

THE BROAD-WINGED HAWK TYPICALLY HUNTS FROM A PERCH. ITS DIET INCLUDES SMALL ANIMALS AND THE OCCASIONAL REPTILE.

Wrens

- Small and chunky
- Slender bill, often curved slightly
- Tail typically short and upright

DEVELOPING YOUR OBSERVATION SKILLS

Observation is the key to being a good birder and to having fun. Developing your skills requires a little bit of patience. I don't know one birder who didn't have to work at improving their observation skills.

Being patient and noticing every aspect of the bird is the first step in developing your skills. Note the shape, size, and color. Determine the length of legs and the shape of the bill. When I first see a bird, I make a list of everything I see. I note the field

SNOW GEESE ARE USUALLY SEEN IN LARGE GROUPS. PAIRS TYPICALLY MATE FOR LIFE AND BREED WHEN THEY ARE ABOUT THREE YEARS OLD.

UNDERSTANDING BIRD BEHAVIOR

A birds behavior can give you a lot of clues to its identity. Watching how birds fly, how they stand, and how they eat can often help you figure out just what kind of birds they are. You can often identify a bird by its displays in courtship or by the way it flies as it searches for its food. Is the bird on the ground, or does it appear to be climbing up the side of a tree? Is it gliding through the sky as though it doesn't need its wings, or is it flapping while flying in an up-and-down motion? Answering some basic questions can help you learn to identify the birds better.

THE BALTIMORE ORIOLE'S PREFERENCE FOR BUILDING HANGING NESTS IN TALL TREES SURROUNDING OPEN AREAS MAKES IT A COMMON SIGHT IN SUBURBAN NEIGHBORHOODS AND PARKS.

marks, wing bars, or any other detail that may help me identify the bird.

In addition to physical characteristics, don't forget to notice its behavior. There may be important clues there. Listen to what noises the bird is making. Watch how the bird is behaving. The more you notice about the bird, the more you will remember about it later. It will also be easier to identify that same species of bird the next time you see it.

Sketching birds is a great way to develop observational skills because you may remember more details if you have to draw them. Even a simple sketch can record a lot: specific field marks, bill shape, and length

of legs. You can also draw the birds in your backyard. Don't worry about being perfect; think about the sketches as taking notes, not creating art. In the field, just capture the important features of the bird. You can add written notes to help you remember the details. Make notes about how the bird was behaving and anything unusual. You can also write what you think the bird was singing or the noise it was making. You can even add color if you really want to capture the birds details. Feel free to add formal entries once you have returned home. Think of your sketchpad as a birding journal and an education tool.

WHY BIRD BEHAVIOR MATTERS

Most good field guides will describe what kind of behaviors birds exhibit. Learning them will help you identify them.

Some birds are well-known for how they behave. Famous for its displays, the killdeer uses a distraction if it thinks a predator is getting too close to its nest or young. The bird droops one of its wings on the ground and walks away to lure you from its nest. Once you are far enough away, it gathers up its wing and flies off. This display is also done by other ground-nesting birds such as sandpipers, nighthawks, and shorebirds.

THE SCISSOR-TAILED FLYCATCHER IS OFTEN SEEN PERCHED ON WIRES ALONG THE ROADSIDE. ITS LONG TAIL IS VERY NOTICEABLE AS IT FLIES.

STARTING A LIFE LIST

Life birds are birds you see for the first time, and your life list is the list of birds you've seen since you began birdwatching. Some birders keep a list separated by yard, city, state, region, country, or even year. Some of the lists are meant to be competitive and come with bragging rights, and some are simply for fun. My life list is an old *North American Birds* checklist someone gave me years ago that I pull out every once in a while to update. Bird names change from time to time, and I scratch one off and replace it with the new one if need be. When I first started my life list—years after I actually stared birding—I never put the date I saw the bird for the first time, but recently I started tracking more of the new species I find as I travel to new places. Lists can be fun, but, for me, they are personal and are for my benefit only.

Some birds do things that distinguish them easily from other, similar birds. For example, the phoebe is a tail-bobbing flycatcher. It will fly around catching insects and then land on a twig, immediately bobbing its tail up and down. Northern mockingbirds do what is called wing-flashing. The bird slowly raises its outstretched wings in a series of jerky motions. Mockingbirds also imitate the songs and calls of other birds. They typically repeat each song or call three or more times before changing tunes. You may think you have three or four different birds in one tree until you realize that it is a mockingbird. Males will often sing into the night if they haven't found a mate or if the night sky is very light.

A great way to watch a bird's behavior is to set up a backyard habitat and bird-feeding station. Watch for the nuthatch as it comes to the feeder, chooses a seed, and flies away. The nuthatch will often pry the seed open by sticking it in the bark of a tree. Chickadees come to the feeder, take a seed, place it in their feet, and break it open with their bill. Watch as both of these birds carefully select their seeds. They actually weigh the seeds as they sift through them to see which one is the heaviest.

If you have never set up a birdbath or watched birds bathe, it is well worth the effort. Hummingbirds will fly through a mister set up at the bath. Goldfinches and chickadees will walk to the tip of a dripper and drink from the spout. If you have never seen a group of baby robins take a bath, you are missing a wonderful sight! The most important rule about bird behavior is to take your time and observe it. Birds are fascinating and learning what to watch for is half the fun.

YOU PROBABLY ALREADY RECOGNIZE MORE BIRDS THAN YOU KNOW THE NAME OF.

STARTING A BIRDING JOURNAL

Keeping a birding journal or life list can add to your enjoyment. One value of keeping a list of the birds you have seen is that you have a clear record. Another is that it can

KEEPING A LIFE LIST OF BIRDS CAN HELP YOU REMEMBER ALL THE SPECIES YOU HAVE SEEN.

be fun to look at. There are many different types of lists that birdwatchers keep. Some, like me, just have a life list of the names of birds I have observed. Others have a life list that records where and when they have seen the bird. Some birders have multiple lists that include a list of backyard birds, city birds, state birds, country birds, and so on. Some even have year lists. Most people keep a trip list of the birds they have seen while traveling.

There are some basic rules to making a life list. You are supposed to record only birds you have seen since you started your list. Captive or caged birds don't count. Only list birds that you have actually identified. You can list birds you have heard, though some birders don't think you can be sure unless you actually see it. While many birders can become competitive about their lists, the list is yours to do with as you like.

Getting into the habit of taking field notes can be beneficial, not only because you may get more enjoyment out of doing it, but also because you can document what you see. It is not always easy to carry a notebook or camera into the field, so journal entries can help you track your experiences. They are a great way to relive your birding experiences and to share them with others. Keeping records can also be useful if others are interested in learning about a certain area where you regularly bird. Sometimes rare birds or rare circumstances related to birds have been documented in personal journals and been helpful to ornithologists later.

TOP LEFT: SUMMER TANAGERS ARE FOUND IN HIGH TREE FOLIAGE AND CAN CATCH INSECTS IN MIDAIR. TOP RIGHT: THE GREEN KINGFISHER IS A SMALL KINGFISHER WITH A VERY LARGE BILL. BOTTOM RIGHT: VISITOR CENTERS ARE A TERRIFIC SOURCE OF BIRDING INFORMATION. BOTTOM LEFT: ONCE NEARLY EXTINCT, THE WOOD STORK IS THE LARGEST WADING BIRD IN NORTH AMERICA.

TOP: THE ANHINGA IS A LONG-NECKED BIRD OFTEN SEEN PERCHED ON DEAD BRANCHES ABOVE THE WATER, WITH ITS WINGS SPREAD OUT TO DRY. BOTTOM: KEEP YOUR FIELD GUIDE HANDY FOR EASY IDENTIFICATION.

You can make your journal or notebook as detailed or fancy as you want it to be. If you want to share it with others, that is your decision. You may find that your children or grandchildren might be interested in sharing your journals. Creating a journal or notebook can enhance your hobby of watching birds.

There is always the chance we will misidentify a bird, and that is all part of the learning process. My husband called me one day while I was out of town on a trip. He was pleased to tell me that he saw a hairy woodpecker at the new feeder he had placed in our yard. The next day he said he was mistaken, and he thought it was a downy woodpecker instead. When I returned home, he told me that he kept seeing the bird and couldn't figure out which one it was. Finally, he saw both at the feeder and one was a hairy and the other, a downy!

The downy and hairy woodpeckers are almost carbon copies of each other. The hairy woodpecker is larger than the downy, but many people find this hard to know for sure. The best way to recognize the downy—other than its size—is that the bill is about half the length of the head. The hairy's bill is almost as long as the head. You will be able to tell how long the bill is compared to the head even if you don't see the birds side by side. Their tail feathers also offer a clue as to which bird is which. The hairy woodpecker's outer feathers are pure white, and the downy usually has black spots along the sides of the white outer tail feathers.

THE BALI MYNAH IS A CRITICALLY ENDANGERED BIRD NATIVE TO BALI FOUND ONLY IN THE BALI BARAT NATIONAL PARK.

There are times when you may not always be sure of your identification. How do you know if you have assigned the right name to a bird? Unless you take very good notes or photographs and can share them with another birder, you may not know if you have misidentified a bird. Even if you use all the tools of the trade—field guides, special books designed for hard-to-identify birds, spotting scopes, your knowledge of bird characteristics and bird behavior—you still may not get the identification right. Practice helps, but there are experts in the field who sometimes incorrectly identify a bird or two. The more you bird and the more experience you gain, the fewer mistakes you will probably make. Meanwhile, just learn all you can and enjoy.

CHAPTER SIX

GETTING THE MOST OUT OF YOUR EQUIPMENT

HOW TO USE YOUR BASIC BIRDING EQUIPMENT LIKE A PRO

- *Binoculars*

- *Spotting scopes*

- *Sound equipment*

- *Clothing and equipment*

Birdwatching can be an easy hobby, enjoyed without any special equipment or training. You can simply take a walk and watch for birds. Having some equipment, such as binoculars, spotting scopes, cameras, sound equipment, special clothing and more, can enhance your experience.

There are times I have taken a walk and chosen not to take my binocular or field guide. My intent was just to listen to the sounds of the birds and nature. Invariably I wished I had brought my binocular so I could get a closer look at some of the birds. If you want to enhance your experience of birdwatching and improve your ability to identify the birds, a good binocular is indispensable.

BINOCULARS

For many people, purchasing a binocular is a once-in-a-lifetime event, and they can last a lifetime if you choose them wisely. Get one that fits your budget and that you feel comfortable using. You may find that once you really get into birdwatching, you might purchase additional binoculars and will probably invest in a scope. All of your equipment depends on how much birding you plan to do and where.

THERE ARE MANY DIFFERENT KINDS OF BINOCULARS. WORK WITH A KNOWLEDGEABLE
SALESPERSON WHO CAN HELP YOU SAMPLE THE FIT AND FEATURES OF EACH.

I am not sure it is important to understand all the technical terms and mechanics of optics equipment. However, understanding the basics will help you choose and enjoy your binocular more. Don't fret. There will not be a test at the end of this chapter. If you take the time to look through a variety of binoculars and take some for a test run, you will be happy with your selection.

All binoculars are labeled with two numbers separated by an "x." The average binocular is a 7x35. The first number is the magnification—the power of the binocular. The higher the magnification, the closer the image looks. In a 7x35 binocular, the bird is seven times closer than it really is. The second number, 35, indicates the diameter of the objective lens—the light-gathering lens—in millimeters. This lets light enter the binocular, resulting in a brighter image.

Purchasing Tips

There are many models available, and you will want to consider a number of things when you choose your binocular:

- Price—What is your budget? Binoculars come in all price ranges and the quality of the optics and workmanship varies. The higher-priced models are almost always water- and shockproof, and come with substantial warranties. You can spend $100 for an economical model that can serve your needs or you can spend $1,000 or more for a high-quality, top-performing model. There are well-made models in the mid-range price category. Regardless of your budget, try binoculars in all price

categories before selecting one that's right for you. Buy the best one you can afford now. You can always upgrade later.

- Size—Will you be okay with a large binocular or do you want a compact that can fit into your purse or pocket? I have never really been fond of compacts, especially for the beginner or children. Their field of view is often too narrow and that makes it harder to find the birds. My husband, however, likes the compacts and is just as satisfied with them as he is with my Swaroskvi 8x30 or the Eagle Optic Ranger 10x42.

HAVING A COMFORTABLE STRAP ON YOUR BINOCULAR WILL REDUCE NECK FATIGUE.

YOU DON'T HAVE TO OWN VARIOUS BINOCULARS TO BE A BIRDWATCHER, BUT IT WILL ENHANCE YOUR BIRDWATCHING PLEASURE.

- Weight—Do you want very light weight or something slightly heavier? Generally, the higher the power, the heavier the binocular.

- Armored or Not—Most models of binoculars are armored with a rubbery outer material to withstand rough treatment and provide a solid grip.

- Glasses—Do you wear glasses? You will want to find a binocular that will accommodate your glasses. Most have adjustable eye cups that allow you to get your eyes closer to the lens. This helps you see through the lenses better and have the widest possible field of view. I sometimes wear glasses, and my binoculars have adjustable eye cups that twist, as opposed to folding down.

- Face Size—Is your face small or large? Binoculars will need to adjust to your face.

- Hands—Are your hands small or large? You need to easily find and adjust the focus. Nothing is more frustrating than having to struggle with bringing something into focus, just to find it has flown away.

- Warranties—Does the binocular have a good warranty? Be sure you understand exactly what the terms are, so you won't be disappointed when something goes wrong. Some stores will take care of shipping them back to the company for repair and may even have loaner binoculars; others expect you to fend for yourself. Buying your optics from a reputable company will make any repairs or problems much easier to handle.

Understanding Some Basic Terms

Magnification

The higher the magnification of the binocular, the larger the birds will appear. However, more magnification can come at a price: You may find your eyes tire more easily, and you may have a hard time keeping the binocular steady. Scopes are placed on a tripod because the magnification is so high. Higher-magnification binoculars also tend to be heavier but can be beneficial for some birding conditions, such as viewing hawks and waterbirds.

Waterproof

There are different levels of how "waterproof" binoculars will be. Some are waterproof, which is important if you bird on the water or in wet conditions; some are water-resistant and/or fog proof, which is helpful if you get caught out in the rain. Some may not be resistant to water at all. Truly waterproof binoculars are literally submersible, and any water damage should be handled under the manufacturer's warranty.

Close Focus

The close focus, or near focus, of a binocular varies. If you plan to watch butterflies or insects you need to be close to what you are watching. Choose one with a low close-focus number.

Coated Lenses

A thin layer of an anti-reflection coating is applied to the glass surface. More light will pass through to reach your eye. Top-of-the-line binoculars are made with the

THE BARN OWL IS FOUND IN NEARLY ALL WORLDWIDE LOCALES, AND HISSES RATHER THAN HOOTS.

highest-quality lenses, fully multicoated with state-of-the-art materials for maximum light-loss prevention.

Nitrogen Purged

Most waterproof binoculars are nitrogen-purged, which means the air in the binocular is replaced with nitrogen. This prevents mold and mildew of lenses and prisms. Extreme humidity can create internal fogging, but, most of the time, this moisture dissipates on its own in a matter of minutes.

Diopter Adjuster

The diopter adjustment allows for separate adjustment of the focus for each eyepiece.

Named for the way they search for food, Ruddy Turnstones turn over small stones and pebbles along rocky shorelines.

This is done to compensate for differences between eyes.

Field of View

When you look through your binocular, the widest dimension you can see is known as the field of view. Wide fields of view are preferred over narrow ones, especially for spotting a moving bird. This measurement may be listed on the binocular in either degrees or feet, measured at 1,000 yards (914 m). One degree equals 52.5 feet (16 m)/1,000 yards (914 m). This measurement is usually listed in degrees. The higher the number of degrees, the wider the field of view. Compact binoculars usually do not have a wide field of view.

CEDAR WAXWINGS ARE OFTEN SEEN SITTING IN TREES PASSING BERRIES BACK AND FORTH TO EACH OTHER.

Exit Pupil

A useful gauge of brightness is called the exit pupil. This can be determined by dividing the size of the binocular's objective lens by its power. The higher the second number of the binocular, the wider the view and the more light you will have.

Eye Relief

The eye relief of binoculars is the distance from where the eye is placed at which the exit pupil is approximately the same size as the eye's pupil. Eye relief can be particularly important for eyeglass wearers because the eye is typically further from the eye piece, which means a longer eye relief is needed in order to see the entire field of view. Without a long eye relief, eyes can tire more easily.

Considering all the points above will help you find a binocular that will fit and work best for you. Go to a store that has a nice selection of optics and explore. Try a bunch of them on and make sure you look through them outdoors, but not through a window as that could distort your view. Visiting a nature center that has a bird observation room with binoculars is another good way to test optics. Many nature centers offer loaner binoculars on their guided bird walks. Look at what other people are using, and don't be afraid to ask questions about how they like their binoculars and what they find most beneficial when they watch birds.

Focusing Binoculars

Being able to focus on the birds is important for getting the best use out of your binocular. You will need to adjust the diopter to compensate for differences between your eyes. Cover the right lens with your hand and adjust the knob. Cover the left lens next and adjust the knob again. This should make the image clear once you focus on an object. Adjust your binocular so the eyepieces line up properly with your eyes, and find the focus wheel with your index finger. Focus on a distant object such as a sign with very small letters. Try to do this outside where you don't have a distorted view. Adjust the focus wheel until the letters, or whatever you are looking at, are clear and in focus. Check the field of view and remember the wider, the better. If you can't hold the binocular steady, find it awkward to adjust the focus wheel, or see blackness or double images, this binocular may not be for you. Do the same with any model you're considering.

BEING COMFORTABLE WHILE YOU ARE WATCHING BIRDS WILL MAKE YOUR EXPERIENCE MUCH MORE ENJOYABLE.

Care of Binoculars

Use common sense in care and maintenance. Don't use your shirttail or pocket tissue to clean your optics. These fibers may contain material which will scratch the coatings on the lenses. Before using a lens cleaning tool like a Lens Pen or lens-cleaning tissue, blow off any visible dust or dirt. Gently wipe off any remaining marks or spots with the special lens cloth or tool. You can remove stubborn things like dried water spots by lightly fogging the binocular lens with your breath.

In addition to keeping the lenses of your binocular clean, keep the eyecups and focus mechanisms free of debris. You also want to check your neck strap and its

THE LONG-BILLED CURLEW IS ONE OF OUR LARGEST SHOREBIRDS. IT WINTERS IN THE SOUTHERN UNITED STATES BUT HAS DECLINED DUE TO LOSS OF HABITAT.

clasps for wear and tear. You don't want your binocular to come loose and drop to the ground. I like to own more than one binocular in the event I need to send one off for repair.

When you are not using your binocular, keep it in the case or away from dust and debris. Most come with lens caps, and while you can place the lens caps on the binocular each time you use it, you may miss a bird while fussing with the lens caps. It is probably more convenient and just as good to place the caps on when you put your binocular away until you use it next. Your binocular is an investment, and you want to take good care of it.

Shopping Tips

- Don't be afraid to test binoculars. Try out as many as you can.

- Ask other birders or nature center staff and volunteers for recommendations regarding what to buy and where.
- Consider searching on the Internet to check features and prices, and then head to the store.
- Try models in all price ranges.
- Buy the binocular that feels right for you; don't be pressured into buying something you don't really want. If you're not convinced, try another store or come back in a few days.

The following chart is designed to give you an idea of the price range and features of various binoculars. When considering which binocular to purchase, take some time to look at the features you want and give as many as possible a test drive before deciding what is best for you.

BINOCULAR MODELS AND FEATURES

MODEL	FEATURES	COMMENTS
ECONOMICAL: UNDER $200		
Bushnell Birder 8x40		Good for children
Bushnell Excursion 10x42	Waterproof, nitrogen purged, fully-coated lenses	Great for use on water
Nikon Action 7x35	Multicoated lenses, rubber-coated	Large center wheel focus
Nikon Action 8x40	Multicoated lenses, rubber-coated	Wide field of view, great price for the optics
MID-RANGE: $200 TO $750		
Swift Audubon ED 8½x44	Waterproof, fully-coated lenses, rubber-coated	Wide field of view, excellent optics for the price
Eagle Optics Ranger SRT 8x42	Waterproof, fogproof, fully-coated lenses	Nice field of view, easy-to-adjust focus, close focus to 5 ft.
Eagle Optics Ranger SRT 10x50	Waterproof, fogproof, fully-coated lenses	Nice field of view, easy-to-adjust focus
Nikon Monarch ATB Binocular 8x36	Waterproof, fogproof, rubber armor, fully-coated lenses	Compact and lightweight with large focus wheel
Nikon Premier SE 8x32	Water-resistant, multilayered lens coating	Small binoculars, lightweight
Bushnell Elite e2 8x42 Binocular	Waterproof, fogproof, multicoated	Twist-up eyepieces, bright, nice field of view
TOP-OF-THE-LINE: $750 AND UP		
Zeiss Victory 8x32	Waterproof, fogproof, multi-coated lenses, rubber-coated	Transferable lifetime warranty, quality optics
Leica Ultravid 8x32	Waterproof, fogproof, lightweight, multicoated lenses, armored	Excellent lifetime "no-fault" warranty, quality optics, generous field of view
Swarovski EL 10x42	Waterproof, fogproof, multicoated lenses, magnesium housed	Excellent warranty and service, quality optics
Nikon Premier LX L 10x42	Waterproof, fogproof, fully-multicoated lenses	Long eye relief, lightweight for the size, quality optics

SPOTTING SCOPES

Binoculars are great for helping birders get a closer look at the birds they are watching. There are times, however, when birds are at greater distances and cannot be easily identified. This distance may be when you are birdwatching in a grassland area, over water, on the beach, or across a field. Using a spotting scope is helpful then. Because of the higher magnification of a scope, they typically sit on a tripod.

Magnification or power of the scope depends on the eyepiece and the design. By exchanging eyepieces, you can increase or decrease the magnification of the spotting scope. Zoom-spotting scopes have a single, built-in eyepiece to give you a range of magnifications without the need to change eyepieces.

Under normal conditions—average light, no rain, and a reasonable distance from the birds—a magnification of 20 to 35 times is probably the most useful and satisfying range to use with spotting scopes. The maximum magnification is typically 50 to 60 times. Magnification any higher than 50 or 60 may produce fuzzy images and can add to your frustration of not being able to identify the bird you are trying to focus on.

Most scope lenses are coated; some are coated on one side of each lens, but most are coated on each side and on every lens. The better the quality of the lens coatings, the brighter and the higher the contrast of the image will be. Fully multicoated lenses are the best quality you can choose.

Scopes come with several options of how the eyepiece is positioned. Some are straight, so you look straight into the barrel of the scope. Other scopes have an angled eyepiece so you are looking at an angle into the eyepiece. The straight eyepiece position features a more natural line of sight that may be helpful when following wildlife. Because this is the way most people look into binoculars, it is often easier for a beginner to use. The straight eyepiece also works well when you are positioned on an elevated platform looking down. The angled eyepiece position also has its advantages. By using an angled eyepiece position,

SPOTTING SCOPES SET ON A TRIPOD ARE VERY HELPFUL WHEN OBSERVING WATER BIRDS, AND OTHER SPECIES, AT A DISTANCE.

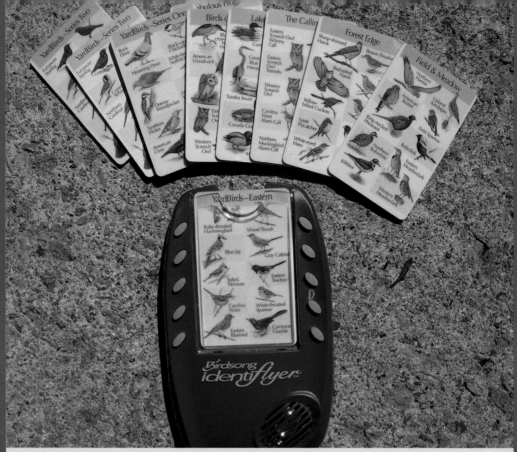

THE IDENTIFLYER IS A SIMPLE AND INEXPENSIVE GADGET TO HELP BEGINNERS
LEARN BASIC BIRD SONGS AND CALLS.

RECOGNIZING BIRD SONGS

The more birds you hear, the more birds you will see. Recognizing and identifying bird songs and calls can help you find and identify birds. Once you learn the basic calls of some of the birds in your own backyard or local park, you may hear these birds in other places you go birding. Bird sounds are divided into songs and calls, though some birds make sounds with their wings. Songs are melodies of musical notes. Songs, done mostly by males, are usually associated with attract-ing a mate or proclaiming territory. Calls are usually used to vocalize warnings or threats and perhaps to communicate in ways we humans don't understand. Calls tend to be short and simple. The songs of birds vary and there are some birds that have a number of songs they sing regularly. There are some birds that don't really have a song of their own and they mimic sounds they learn from other birds, and sometimes sounds that aren't actually bird songs at all!

you can adjust your tripod to a shorter height, and it is easier to share your scope with other birdwatchers because you don't have to adjust the height of the tripod much.

Scopes do not take the place of binoculars, and there will be situations when you feel you may need both a scope and a binocular on your birdwatching trip. It really depends on where you are birding and what type of habitat you plan to watch birds in. Using a scope in a wooded area is not practical nor is it necessary. If you are planning to go to an area that has a pond or field area, taking a scope will enable you to watch the birds that may be on the other side of the pond.

SOUND EQUIPMENT

Being able to recognize the songs and calls of birds will help you find and identify them. All bird species have their own sounds, with the exception of birds such as the mockingbird. There are a variety of tools available to help you learn the songs and calls. Go slowly at first. Focus on the birds you will most likely see in your backyard or wherever you plan to take your beginning bird walks.

Once you have learned some of the most common bird calls you will encounter in your day-to-day life or in your local park, you can branch out into more birds. To help learn some of the more common bird calls, you can put phrases to their sounds. For example the American robin sings "cheerily, cheerily, cheery–o" and chickadees basically sing their name "chickadee dee dee dee." Cardinals sing a "pretty bird, pretty bird" song. The jays often call their name with a

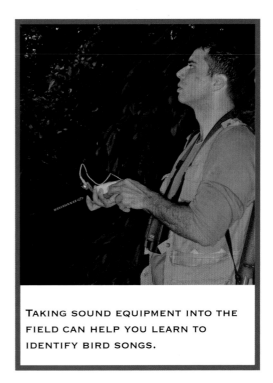

TAKING SOUND EQUIPMENT INTO THE FIELD CAN HELP YOU LEARN TO IDENTIFY BIRD SONGS.

"jay, jay, jay." Learning to associate the bird songs and calls with phrases should make it easier for you to remember them.

Audio CDs

Audio CDs are a great way to start learning the songs and calls of birds. There are CDs specifically designed for backyard birds and some designed to cover specific birds. Most of these are divided into eastern and western birds. Other CDs have a national focus and separate the birds into family groups to help the birdwatcher categorize the birds more easily. Some have booklets that enable the birder to follow along as the bird names are announced and then the song or call played. Some of these also have a section that enables the birder to play the songs and then test their knowledge.

ARTIFICIAL CAVITIES ARE SOMETIMES INSERTED INTO TREES TO PROVIDE SAFE PLACES FOR BIRDS TO NEST.

The following is a list of some available CDs.

Birding by Ear, Eastern/Central, by Richard K. Walton and Robert W. Lawson provides great recordings of the eastern birds of North America. *Birding by Ear* points out exactly what to listen for to tell one bird from another, helping to eliminate trial and error. Designed as a companion to the *Peterson Field Guide to Eastern Birds* these songs are easily applied in the field. Also available on audio cassette.

Birding by Ear, Western, by Richard K. Walton and Robert W. Lawson provides great recordings of the western birds of North America. *Birding by Ear* points out exactly what to listen for to tell one bird from another, helping to eliminate trial and error. Designed as a companion to the *Peterson Field Guide to*

Western Birds these songs are easily applied in the field. Also available on audio cassette.

More Birding by Ear, Eastern/Central, by Richard K. Walton and Robert W. Lawson. This set will teach you the eastern warblers and many other birds that are not contained on the first *Eastern/Central Birding By Ear* CD. Also available in audiocassette.

Peterson Field Guides, Eastern Bird Songs, by Roger Tory Peterson. This CD contains great recordings that follow the *Peterson Field Guide to Eastern Birds*. Songs and calls for over 250 species are included. Also available on audiocassette.

Peterson Field Guides, Western Bird Songs, by Roger Tory Peterson. Great recordings that follow the Peterson's Field Guide to the Birds West of the Rockies. Songs and calls for over 250 species are included. Also available on audiocassette.

Stokes Field Guide to Bird Songs: Eastern Region, by Lang Elliott with Donald and Lillian Stokes. This CD contains 374 sound recordings of eastern birds of North America. Most of these songs were recorded by Lang Elliott—one of my favorite bird sound recorders. A booklet with descriptions of the bird songs and calls accompanies the CD. Also available as an audiocassette.

Stokes Field Guide to Bird Songs: Western Region, by Lang Elliott with Donald and Lillian Stokes. This Western Edition of the Stokes

Bird Song series follows the same format and pattern as the Eastern Region guide. The main author of this collection is Kevin J. Colver. Also available as an audiocassette.

Computer CD-ROMs

CD-ROMs are a great way to learn the bird sounds because you are able to view the birds and listen to their songs at the same time. These are a great way to explore the birds because they offer the ability to focus on the birds you are most interested in learning about.

Birds of North America with Roger Tory Peterson, presents over 700 North American bird species and their songs and calls in full multimedia. This CD contains the text and detailed artwork of the *Peterson Field Guides,* along with photographs, videos, bird songs, and range maps. The "Bird Finder" search tool helps you identify birds based on color, size, region, and habitat, and includes a life list to help you track the birds you are observing as you take your birdwatching trips.

National Audubon Society CD-ROM includes pictures, sounds, games, and more for Mac and PC. Learn bird songs, habitats, and behavior. Practice your identification skills.

Thayers FeederWatcher's Guide to Backyard Birds CD-ROM includes 135 birds seen at feeders in North America. This program includes some spring migrants that may not be common but may visit your yard. It is a basic CD-ROM, and you will find it helpful to get you started.

Thayers Birds of North America CD-ROM. Thayer worked with Cornell Lab of Ornithology to produce this CD-ROM containing 926 birds of the U.S. and Canada. You can identify birds by color, size, habitat, location, and even by sound. It has over 2,700 color photos, and a spectrogram shows the voice pattern of the birds—this is fun, but not necessary for you to learn the birdsongs and calls. Range maps as well as 90 videos show birds and their behavior. You can also export songs to an MP3 player such as an iPod.

Audio websites

An excellent way to explore the bird sounds without investing a lot of money is websites. These sites often offer additional resources and links to other interesting sites. The Internet

AUDIO AND COMPUTER CDS CAN ENHANCE YOUR BIRDING EXPERTISE.

can provide many great tools in your quest to learn more about birds. I prefer organizations that contribute to research and conservation.

One of my two favorite sites is the Patuxent Wildlife Research Center where you can find the "Patuxent—Bird Songs" section which not only includes the songs and calls of birds, but also a Bird Identification Center and seasonal bird checklists. This site also offers a bird quiz to test your identification knowledge. (http://www. mbr-pwrc.usgs.gov/id/songlist.html)

Cornell Lab of Ornithology Macaulay Library boasts the world's largest sound collection online. The site offers spectrograms and videos. You can also search for behaviors and explore Google Maps for the

THE FLORIDA SCRUB JAY IS FOUND ONLY IN THE RARE SCRUB OAK PORTIONS OF FLORIDA. IT IS A COOPERATIVE BREEDER, WITH SOME OFFSPRING HELPING WITH THE NEXT GENERATION.

birds' ranges. (http://www.birds.cornell. edu/MacaulayLibrary/search/index.html)

Other Options

One of the great things about birding is there is always new and fun gear to play with. Here are two favorites.

- The Birdsong IdentiFlyer—Made by For the Birds, the IdentiFlyer is a battery-operated handheld device that has interchangeable song cards. The 25 SongCards contain 250 bird songs along with small color illustrations. They are arranged by habitat, making it easy to recognize birds in your area. While, the IdentiFlyer doesn't have great sounds, it is easy for the beginner to use and is not a huge investment of time and money.

- The birdJam—While it is possible to load bird songs onto an iPod, the birdJam (www.birdjam.com) has built-in features to organize your bird songs. It is very lightweight, fits in the palm of one hand, and operates with a single finger. It includes 650 bird songs and eliminates bulky and hard-to-use tapes and CDs. Just scroll, click, and listen to find any bird song. BirdJam includes 100 common bird songs and photos for iPods as well as other MP3 players. You will need a computer with an operating system that supports the playing of MP3 files, an iPod or other MP3 player that supports color photography, and a current music management system such as iTunes, Windows Media Player, RealPlayer, or something similar installed on your computer, with fast Internet access (not dial-up) for ease of downloading bird songs/photos.

CLOTHING AND EQUIPMENT

A question I am often asked is whether there is special equipment and clothing for the person who watches birds. The answer is yes. Many types of clothing used for hiking, biking, walking, and other outdoor activities are fine for birdwatching in the field. There are, however, a number of manufacturers and stores that offer a wide variety of options, many with garments and accessories specifically geared for birders.

The important thing for birders to consider when choosing clothing and equipment is where and when you will be birding and how much you want to take along. The clothes and equipment you choose should be functional, comfortable, and be able to withstand various weather conditions. Also, jackets, vests, and packs need to hold all the equipment you plan to carry.

While in the field, the fabric of any item of clothing you are wearing is critical, especially if the weather changes unexpectedly. Fabrics that have muted colors, make as little noise as possible, are durable, and are able to withstand rain and wind are key. Clothing that is lightweight and easily packed is also a plus. Other features to look for are pockets large enough for binoculars, field guides, and other gear. Padded shoulders—to ease the weight of carried items—are a good feature in vests and jackets.

MAKE SURE TO SELECT THE RIGHT EQUIPMENT FOR TERRAIN AND WEATHER CONDITIONS.

Modern technology has produced many terrific fabrics that breathe, keep away moisture, insulate the body, and feel good against your skin. Cotton is a great fabric, but not always practical. It is best to dress in layers, starting with a fabric such as polypropylene, Thermax, Thinsulate, or silk. In cold or wet weather the next layer should be wool or wool blend, or even fleece. The last layer in cold weather should be a wind- or water-resistant jacket. Gore-Tex is a terrific fabric that is waterproof, windproof, and breathable. Look for this fabric to ensure comfort and quality. If the weather is really cold, you may want to bring long underwear, and make sure you wear socks. I like to layer my socks with a polypropylene liner and a Smartwool or all wool sock.

The type of clothing you wear will be influenced by the habitat you plan to visit.

For bird watching on a beach, short pants and short-sleeved tops are suitable, but remember to bring a hat and sun block. A lightweight vest with room for a bottle of water, a field guide, and a pad of paper will eliminate the need for a backpack. Sandals can be used when on the beach, but bring sneakers if you plan to walk great distances. When birding for species found along forest edges and in the forest, it is advisable to wear closed shoes. Long pants will help protect against thorns, insects, and poison ivy; some long pants have zippers on the leg that allow you to remove the bottom half. This is great when you start out on a cold morning and it warms up later.

There are many hats suitable for wearing while watching birds. Some have special flaps that fold down to help protect the back of your neck from the sun and insects. Many companies manufacture hats for birders, but Tilley hats are a standout. They are guaranteed

HAVING THE RIGHT HAT WILL HELP PROTECT YOU FROM THE RAVAGES OF THE SUN OR INCLEMENT WEATHER.

for life, come in a wide variety of sizes and styles, repel rain, protect against the sun, have a secret pocket and a security strap, and they float. The Tilley company is so sure you will enjoy your hat, that if you lose it you can purchase another at half price.

Vests are a staple for most birders. When choosing one, try them on over a jacket or under rain gear. The Birders' Buddy Vest has a lot of room and is lightweight, durable, and fits a variety of body types. The pockets are big and fasten shut, with the side open for ventilation. There is also a roomy pocket on the back to carry a field guide, lunch, or a camera. Big Pockets vests have plenty of large pockets that will accommodate binoculars, books, and more. They feature a zippered security pocket on the inside of one of the chest pockets, and the shoulders are padded to improve comfort while carrying items on your shoulder. Additionally, there is a ring on the front for sunglasses or anything with a strap.

For seasonal birding, look for jackets that use fabrics such as Gore-Tex, which is waterproof, breathable, and wind resistant. A jacket should be your top layer unless you choose to wear a vest over it. A removable hood is helpful, and make sure the jacket has adjustable sleeves at the wrists and a belt that can be tightened when the wind is cold and blustery.

While many products such as backpacks and fanny packs may say they are geared toward birders, you really have to test them out. What you choose depends on where you are going birding and for how long. If you plan to be out only for a morning or a day trip, a fanny pack or small pack may be enough. Take your field guide and binocular to the store when shopping and make sure you have room for all the items you will take along.

Some Fun Items For Birdwatchers

The Cobber® Neck Wrap, made in Australia, is an innovative cooling system using non-toxic crystals which helps cool your neck in hot climates. Soak the Cobber® in cold water for 30 minutes and it will stay cool for several days.

SuperEar is a personal sound enhancer that magnifies the sounds in the field. Stereo headphones are included, and, if you have trouble hearing the birds, this may be a way to highlight the songs. While not a necessary item, it can enhance your birdwatching.

The National Geographic Handheld Birds & Software is a mobile interactive field guide for birders of all levels. With a price tag of over $500 plus $200 for software, it is expensive. However, it has exceptional pictures, can store bird-sighting data, and can be downloaded to your desktop computer and uploaded to the Cornell Lab of Ornithology for participation in their Citizen Science Research projects.

The Rite-in-the-Rain All Weather Sketch Book and note pads are perfect for keeping notes while you are birding in the field, which can later be transferred to your permanent recording source when you return home.

SIMILAR TO OTHER KINGBIRDS, CASSIN'S KINGBIRD IS USUALLY IDENTIFIED BY ITS DARK BREAST BAND.

The Nomad Adventure Journal is a neat journal pad that is carried in a water-resistant, zippered case. It is minimally packaged, produced with recycled paper and printed with soy-based inks, so it is environmentally friendly.

Remember to explore all your options in finding what works best for you. Specialty bird-feeding stores often carry a wide inventory of birdwatching items, and their staff will often be knowledgeable about new merchandise. Before investing a lot of money in equipment, try asking other birders what works for them. Consider layers of clothing and be sure to test the capacity of the pockets. Make sure you can comfortably carry your field guide, water bottle, snack, or any other gear you want to take along.

CHAPTER SEVEN

UNDERSTANDING BIRD MOVEMENT AND MIGRATION

WHY IT IS IMPORTANT TO BE FAMILIAR WITH BIRD MIGRATION

- *Basics of bird migration*

- *Bird irruptions and sporadic movement*

- *Bird flyways and stopover points*

The migration of birds is the regular seasonal movements between their breeding and wintering regions. It is thought that the general reason birds migrate is because of changes in food supplies. Most of these migrating birds are insect eaters and most insects do not survive the cold North American winters except in larval or egg forms. These birds—called neotropical migrants—remain on their wintering grounds in warmer climates until spring and then migrate back to their breeding grounds in North America to take advantage of the plentiful insect food supply. Birds also migrate to a specific location to breed and raise their young. However, bird migration still holds many mysteries for scientists.

BASICS OF BIRD MIGRATION

Because migration is such a strenuous activity, some birds may not survive the journey. The strongest birds, typically the males, arrive first and stake out prime territories. Most species of returning birds often breed in the same location where they nested the previous year. When the females arrive, they select the males that occupy the best habitats for raising their family. Watching birds in courtship is fascinating as they are often very vocal and in full color. Many species will have one or, possibly two, broods per year.

About 80 percent of the birds found in North America migrate. Some migrate short distances, others long distances. As a general rule, most birds that need open water for feeding migrate. These include wading birds, shorebirds, sandpipers, herons, and geese. They migrate to where they can find a food source, and this may be close to their winter range or far away, depending on the needs of the species. Swallows migrate long distances and form large flocks as they move north. Some birds stay in their breeding and wintering grounds all year,

GREAT EGRETS HAVE A DIET OF MOSTLY FISH. THEY WERE HUNTED FOR THEIR FEATHERS IN THE LATE 1800S BUT ARE NOW PROTECTED.

STUDYING MIGRATION

Scientists conduct various studies and research projects to learn more about migration. Weather radar screens can show big concentrations of birds as they migrate or disperse from their roosts. Hawk watching and migration counts can help scientists collect the numbers of migrating birds. Banding birds also shows where a bird was first banded and how far it traveled. This is a universal technique for studying the movement and survival of birds. The arctic tern probably has the record for the longest migration distance. It flies almost 19,000 miles (30,500 km) each year between its breeding grounds in the arctic and its non-breeding grounds in the Antarctic. The ruby-throated hummingbird, weighing only about as much as a penny, makes a 621 mile (1,000 km) journey from the Yucatán Peninsula across the Gulf of Mexico to the southern coast of the United States.

only moving if it becomes an issue of survival. The American robin, for example, is a short distant migrant, moving only if weather alters its food source.

Some birds seem to have an instinctive ability to migrate, and some learn from their parents. Most birds rely on visual landmarks, such as mountains, rivers, and coasts, for local and long-distance migration. Birds also use one or more of the three types of "compasses" to find their way. They can use the position of the sun during the day and use the setting sun as an indication of due west. Birds that fly at night use celestial navigation, following the patterns of the stars in the sky. Many bird species have tiny grains of a mineral called magnetite just above their nostrils. This mineral may help them to navigate using the Earth's magnetic field, which tells the bird what direction is north.

Swifts and swallows migrate during the day and feed on insects as they fly. In contrast, most songbirds travel at night and spend the daylight hours searching for food and resting. Flocking birds such as waterfowl and soaring birds such as hawks and cranes migrate during the day. These soaring birds often catch thermal updrafts that occur over land. The rising columns of warm air spiraling upward can save the birds' energy because they fly without having to flap their wings. Because so many hawks and cranes stay inland to migrate, you can see them in large numbers

THE RING-NECKED PHEASANT THRIVES IN THE NORTHERN PRAIRIES OF NORTH AMERICA.

as they pass through various areas. In some places, like Hawk Mountain, Pennsylvania, visitors can see 100,000 in one day.

Birdwatching during spring and fall migrations can be spectacular. Keep an eye out for weather conditions that may alter the timing of migration or how the birds move into an area. In the spring, winds from the southwest push birds north on a wave of warm air. This is great weather for birdwatching because you can sometimes follow this weather pattern and go to your favorite warbler watching or migration spot.

Sometimes the weather is not so favorable and the winds are against the birds. They may be forced to wait for better weather. If birds are forced out of the sky, this is often considered a "fall-out." If they fall-out into an area that is considered a "migrant trap"—an area where lots of birds gather because there is not much stopover habitat

THE SUDDEN SPORADIC

MOVEMENT OF

BIRDS DURING

THE WINTER IS

OFTEN AN

AMAZING EVENT

THAT BIRDERS

CAN TAKE

ADVANTAGE OF.

elsewhere—you can see a huge number of birds that under better weather conditions may not be present.

Some organizations track the migration of birds on maps or charts that are posted on the Internet, and rely on birders to keep tabs on the movement of the birds. Other organizations track the movement with radio collars or by banding the birds. The whooping cranes, being reintroduced into the eastern part of North America, are tracked by the Eastern Whooping Crane Partnership. Regular updates about the young cranes following the ultralight planes and their unassisted return flight is tracked by Operation Migration found at www. operationmigration.org. The whooping crane migration, in general, is tracked by the Whooping Crane Conservation Association at www.whoopingcrane.com/wccamigration.htm. The ruby-throated hummingbird spring migration map at www.hummingbirds.net/map.html is a great place to watch the northward movement of this species.

BIRD IRRUPTIONS AND SPORADIC MOVEMENT

Bird migration is generally thought of as a north-and-south movement. Some birds are short-distance migrants and move only as far as they need to find food such as insects, seeds, and berries. Some bird species move only a few miles (kilometers) up and down mountain slopes. "Irruptions" are movements made by birds that go from one area to another due to changes in their environment and the availability of food.

Periodic bird irruptions can add a level of excitement to watching birds in the winter. You may see birds that don't normally winter in your area. Bird listserves buzz with activity when these irruptions happen. The birds most known for winter irruptions are the winter finches, including the pine grosbeak, red crossbill, white-winged crossbill, common redpoll, and evening grosbeak. Other birds will also shift from their typical wintering grounds into other areas: red-breasted nuthatch, Clark's nutcracker, and varied thrush.

THE WHITE-EYED VIREO MALE SINGS ALMOST NONSTOP DURING BREEDING AND NESTING SEASON.

It is believed that irruptions are driven by a lack of food on normal wintering grounds. The availability of seeds and buds consumed by redpolls and pine grosbeaks can vary substantially from year to year. In some years, the food supplies may be adequate, and the birds stay north in the forests during the winter. In other years, circumstances reduce the food produced, and birds need to look for sources elsewhere. For example, common redpolls feed primarily on the catkins produced by birch and alder trees. In an area where catkin production is low, common redpolls leave and irrupt to areas where food is more plentiful.

Some raptors also exhibit irruptive behavior. Northern owls such as the great gray owl and snowy owl sometimes shift from their regular wintering ranges. While most remain in their Canadian homes throughout the winter, in irruptive years large numbers of these species may move into the northern United States. Again, it is thought that the main reason for this shift is a lack of enough food in their wintering home range. Birdwatchers can enjoy this shift and see birds that would not normally be present. Keep an eye out for these irruptions and sporadic movements.

Range expansions are changes in the normal range of a bird species. Usually this is something that is seen over a long period of time, though sometimes birds may expand their ranges within a shorter period. In the last two decades, many scientists and casual bird observers have noticed that many species are arriving to their breeding grounds earlier. Additionally, a significant number of species are also seen farther north than their historical range. It is believed that climate change caused by the buildup of greenhouse gases may be disrupting the timing of migration. Scientists are still asking questions about range expansion, bird irruptions, and sporadic behavior. Visit Chapter Ten to

THE RED-TAILED HAWK IS THE MOST WIDESPREAD OF THE LARGE HAWKS OF NORTH AMERICA.
IT IS COMMONLY SEEN PERCHED ON ROADSIDE POLES AND SOARING OVER FIELDS.

learn more about some of the citizen science projects that can help scientists answer questions about bird movement.

BIRD FLYWAYS AND STOPOVER POINTS

There are four main North American migratory paths, which are called flyways. Flyways are broad areas, like highways, that migratory birds use to fly from particular breeding grounds to wintering grounds and vice versa. The flyways branch off into smaller migratory paths that birds follow to reach their final destination.

The four major North American flyways are the Atlantic, the Mississippi, the Central, and the Pacific. The boundaries of these flyways are not sharply defined, but the Central flyway is used most by birds that make a direct north and south journey. The Atlantic flyway has a stretch of unbroken ocean about 500 miles (800 km) across. This trip over the ocean can be hazardous for birds because there is no place to land. The Mississippi flyway includes a shortcut across the Gulf of Mexico. Sometimes birds have been known to land on ships and oil rigs.

Most songbirds need to stop along their migratory path to feed and rest. These places are typically called stopover sites. Some birds stay at stopover points only to rest and feed and then continue on their journey. Others will stay at stopover sites for weeks at a time. For those birds heading north or south across the Gulf of Mexico, the Gulf coast is an important area for stopover sites. Birds are able to feed and store up fat reserves before they fly over water, and after flying over the

Gulf, birds sometimes land exhausted from their flight. Occassionally birds return to what they thought was a stopover site to find it has disappeared. Without stopover sites along the way to provide food supplies and a place to rest, birds can suffer. Conservation organizations are working to save as many of these places as possible.

PLACES WHERE BIRDS

CAN REST AND REFUEL ARE IMPORTANT DURING THEIR MIGRATION JOURNEYS.

CHAPTER EIGHT

I'M NOT A BEGINNER ANYMORE. NOW WHAT?

TAKING YOUR HOBBY TO THE NEXT LEVEL

- *Honing your observation skills*

- *Learning more*

- *Photographing birds*

- *Extreme birding*

You don't need to be a scientist—or an ornithologist—to have great observational skills. In fact, my stepson and my daughter are terrific at observing things about birds that I don't always notice. My stepson and I were kayaking on a sunny afternoon when he shouted "Look, an eagle's nest!" Sure enough, I looked and there a young eagle sat in a tall tree, begging for food. The parent was sitting in another tree 10 feet (3 m) away trying to coax the baby from the nest. I was clearly not observing the simple signs that would have helped me locate the nest myself. I had seen the adult eagle with the fish, but not "how" the adult was behaving. Had I been paying attention, I would have seen the nest.

HONING YOUR OBSERVATION SKILLS

At the age of four my daughter, Kathleen, was able to locate a crow's nest at her preschool for the Department of Natural Resources, because she observed details others missed. While hiking the year before, she and I had observed a similar nest, and I pointed out the adult birds feeding the baby birds. We watched the adults gather the insects and take them to the begging baby birds. Kathleen remembered the funny noise that the feeding babies made. When the state naturalist asked if I knew where to find a crow's nest with young, I remembered Kathleen saying there was a nest at school. No one else at her school had remembered even seeing the crows.

Honing your observation skills just means paying attention and learning more about the birds you are watching. Birds give us clues about their lives that help us find them and learn more. You can also use your keen observation skills to help name those hard-to-identify birds. These skills will help

RESEARCH TO FIND THE RIGHT PHOTOGRAPHIC EQUIPMENT FOR THE TYPE OF PICTURES YOU WANT TO SHOOT. ASK FOR TIPS FROM MORE EXPERIENCED BIRDERS.

TIPS FOR BIRD PHOTOGRAPHERS

- Be patient
- Practice with your equipment and your camera
- Learn bird behavior so you can anticipate what they will do
- Know a bird's breeding season and feeding preferences
- Find a spot where you regularly observe birds
- Always shoot when you think you have a shot or you may miss it
- Only show your best shots
- Avoid stressing the birds
- Take action shots
- When digiscoping, trust autofocus
- Photograph in good light—back lighting and morning or afternoon light
- Learn from others

DEMOISELLE CRANES ARE THE SMALLEST OF ALL THE CRANES. THEY ARE NATIVE TO CENTRAL AND EASTERN ASIA, TURKEY, AND NORTH AFRICA.

enable you to tell the difference between a hairy woodpecker and a downy woodpecker. You will also be able to learn the difference between the call of a chickadee and a phoebe. When you are driving down the road and a hawk flies in front of you, can you tell if it is a red-tailed hawk or a red-shouldered hawk? Chapter Five details many aspects of bird observation, but by paying close attention to the small details, you will be able to fine-tune your skills and enjoy your hobby more.

LEARNING MORE

I can't think of one birder who says he or she knows all there is to know about birds. Even experienced birders like David Sibley and Kenn Kaufman are constantly learning. David Sibley will spend hours studying the feathers on one bird species or exploring

the different races of the Canada goose. Just when I think I know a bird I have been watching in my backyard for years, I discover something new about it. Most birders have an insatiable desire to learn more about the birds they are watching.

There are a lot of opportunities to learn more about birds. Many local adult education programs and colleges offer ornithology classes. You may be able to take some of these as a noncredit student. Natural history museums, local bird clubs, and nature centers often offer classes on field identification. Many nature centers and museums train volunteers to lead hikes and teach others about birdwatching—this may be a great way to learn more yourself. Many environmental organizations offer extended bird study courses that often include weekend or week-long seminars and workshops. In addition, look

THE LESSER GOLDFINCH IS A TINY BIRD FOUND IN THE AMERICAN SOUTHWEST. IT
SINGS A SWEET SONG WITH A DISTINCTIVE HIGH-PITCHED "TEE-YEE."

for festivals and natural history conferences that have workshops and field trips. Many environmental organizations also offer working vacations where you can work on a specific project as a volunteer and learn more about bird monitoring or banding.

Visiting places like the Cornell Lab of Ornithology or the Smithsonian Zoo and Natural History Museum offers the opportunity of seeing exhibits specifically about birds. Both have birding paths and bird identification materials that enhance your experience at their facilities. Most Audubon Centers and nature centers have specialized bird trails or areas for birdwatchers, and accompanying educational materials. You can also learn without traveling—the Cornell Lab offers a home study course. It is full of interesting and exciting information, and you can work at your own pace.

A great way to learn more about birds is to volunteer for a citizen science project or do volunteer work for a bird conservation organization. Attending a festival, bird ornithology conference, or a weekend workshop can be educational and rewarding. When you enter the world of birdwatching, you never stop learning and you never stop having fun. For more on these programs and organizations, see Chapters Nine and Ten.

LONG LENSES HELP ENSURE YOU WILL GET CLOSE ENOUGH TO THE BIRDS.

PHOTOGRAPHING BIRDS

Photographing birds is a great next step. Bird photography can be fun and challenging. Taking photographs of the birds you see can help you to identify them later if you couldn't in the field. You can create a photo journal of your bird observations while on a trip.

Photographing birds takes the right equipment, patience, and practice. Many people give up because they may not get good results. My husband and I have explored photographing birds and he has given up, even though many of the pictures he has taken aren't too bad. He would rather enjoy watching the birds than setting up photo opportunities. Unlike my husband, I haven't given up entirely. I try to get a good shot that I can use in my slide show presentations or my conservation work.

If you want to get into bird photography, there are a few things you need to know.

Starting simple is best. Begin with your back-yard or a quiet place you know you will find birds, like the local nature center bird-feeding areas. Birds are attracted to a reliable food source near good cover. Finding a spot where you regularly watch birds is a great way to know you will have a subject to photograph.

You can start with a point-and-shoot camera, but it will not offer the best pictures. Consider investing in equipment that will be more reliable and versatile as you expand your photography hobby. Look for a camera that lets you control the exposure by setting the aperture and shutter speed yourself. A high-quality 35mm single lens reflex camera that can allow a telephoto lens to be mounted is a good start.

ALL LEVELS OF BIRDWATCHERS CAN PARTICIPATE IN BIRDING COMPETITIONS.

BIRDING COMPETITIONS

All over North America there are opportunities for birders to participate in some sort of competitive or extreme birding event. Some of these events are created, planned, and carried out by organizations or individuals hoping to raise awareness of an issue or to raise funds for a project or organization. Other times extreme birding events are organized by an individual or a group of people who need to prove something to themselves or to other birders. Maybe they are just plain crazy about watching birds, and they can't help themselves. Anyone can participate in some form of extreme birding. The sky and your imagination is the limit.

For good shots of birds you need good long lenses. A 300 mm lens is great if you can get close enough to the bird. If you are taking shots of birds in your backyard or feeder station where you can get close, you can fill the frame and get a decent shot. If you are taking shots of birds farther away—especially if they are small—you would need a 400 mm or 500 mm lens. Some photographers go to 800 mm. When using a lens that is 400 mm or greater, you need a tripod in order to hold the camera steady.

PHOTOGRAPHY, OR DIGISCOPING, CAN ENHANCE THE PLEASURE OF LEARNING ABOUT BIRDS.

There are many advantages in using digital cameras, because you receive instant feedback on the quality of the image and bad images can be deleted immediately. Images can be transferred directly to a computer for adjustments, and eliminating film can remove the cost of developing it. Thanks to a growing number of adapters that can attach the latest digital point-and-shoot cameras to spotting scopes, called digiscoping, almost anyone can get into bird photography.

To digiscope, all you have to do is hold your camera up to the eyepiece of a tripod-mounted scope and press the shutter release. When you take a photograph using your digital camera and the spotting scope, the camera lens must be centered precisely over the exit pupil and positioned an exact distance from the eyepiece glass. The camera should not move when the shutter is pushed.

Most birders like to use their scopes to look for birds and to take pictures, so they use a camera-to-scope adapter where their camera can be moved on and off the spotting scope quickly and easily. My friends at Eagle Optics (www.eagleoptics.com) have great advice for birders who want to get into digiscoping and I highly recommend giving them a call.

There are several ways to increase your chances of getting some good shots. Be patient and learn your subject. The more you know about the place where you plan to photograph birds and the more you learn about them, the better your shots will be. Blinds can be a great way to get close to your subjects without spooking them. Depending on where you are planning to do your photography, you can use your car as a blind. Birds may consider a nonmoving vehicle less of a threat than a moving pedestrian. With the engine off, your vehicle provides a stable platform. There are commercially available camera mounts made

specifically for vehicles if you need help keeping your scope or camera steady.

As with any blind, however, patience is a necessity. Scouting out a good location is important. Positioning yourself at an open window, behind a table with a tablecloth to hide your movement, or behind a brush pile can all be effective ways to hide from birds. Catching birds conveniently perched on a branch while they are waiting in line at a bird feeder can also yield excellent results.

Whether you plan to become a professional photographer or you just want to document your bird sightings, you can have fun photographing birds. I recommend taking a digiscoping class or photography class. If you don't want to take a formal class, you can ask more experienced birders to give you a few pointers. Taking a class or spending time with a willing photographer will lessen the frustration of getting started. Most important, have fun and, if you are like me, you will leave the professional bird photographs to the professionals.

EXTREME BIRDING

Every spring in Washington D.C., a team of ornithologists from the Smithsonian Institution gets together to watch birds in an attempt to record as many species as possible in one 24-hour period. Crazy? Extreme? Sort of. These ornithologists not only hope to beat the record from the previous year, but they also want to raise funds for the Smithsonian Migratory Bird Center. This money trains the next generation of scientists to study and protect birds throughout the world.

THERE ARE NUMEROUS OPPORTUNITIES FOR BIRDERS TO PARTICIPATE IN SOME SORT OF COMPETITIVE OR EXTREME BIRDING EVENT.

There are different definitions of extreme birding. Some believe it means strenuous and hard core trips to find rare or vagrant birds. Either the conditions are so extreme that reaching a particular bird is difficult, or the bird is so hard to find that it takes extreme effort to locate it. Some birdwatchers find it extreme when a group of birders start birding at midnight and go continuously for the next 24 hours.

The Smithsonian crew feels it is worth the lack of sleep if they can get enough pledges to support their programs. The competition of breaking the record makes it more of a challenge for the team members. They also hope it will make it more interesting for the people donating money to their efforts. Many birdathon teams or individuals who take on such an effort are rewarded through financial contributions and through the recognition they gain.

It is not possible to list all the birdathon, birdwatching, or other competitions. There are a few, however, that are worth mentioning. The Great Texas Birding Classic has a competitive birdwatching tournament held each spring that coincides with spring migration in Texas. The Gulf Coast Bird Observatory and Texas Parks and Wildlife organize the competition to increase the appreciation, understanding, and conservation of birds along the Great Texas Coastal Birding Trail. Every year they raise over $50,000

that goes to conservation, restoration, and land acquisition projects to benefit birds.

The World Series of Birding started in 1984 when the New Jersey Audubon Society challenged birders to participate in a birdwatching contest to raise money for bird conservation. The birders sign up to bird for 24 hours on the second Saturday of each May. The World Series has grown to include many organizations outside of New Jersey that raise money for bird conservation. Every year many teams of birders compete, and millions of dollars have been raised. Each team chooses a conservation project to which their pledged dollars are donated. Teams from the Cornell Lab of Ornithology, Maryland Ornithological Society, and Cape May Bird Observatory regularly compete. Twenty-four hours of nonstop birding is extreme, but the birders and the birds think it is well worth the effort.

NATIVE TO AFRICA, THE BLACKSMITH PLOVER IS FOND OF THE DRY GROUND BESIDE RIVERS AND PONDS.

LORIKEETS ARE MEMBERS OF THE PARROT FAMILY. MOST MATE FOR LIFE AND STAY TOGETHER PREENING AND CARING FOR EACH OTHER.

There are other types of competitive birding. A Big Day is typically a 24-hour period in which birders try to see as many birds as they can in a given geographic area such as a county or a state. It is usually just a fun competition, or it may raise funds for a local project. Another event is The Big Sit. The Big Sit birding competition was a creation of the New Haven Birding Club in Connecticut. It started because the bird club wanted an alternative event to Big Day. The Big Sit differs from other birdathons, like the Big Day, because it limits the geographic area to a very small place, removing the need for transportation or time management. Participants define a 17-foot (5 m) diameter circle and watch birds from this circle all day, counting the number of species they see. The Big Sit birding competition rules allow participants to leave the circle when they need to, but all birds must be sighted or heard from within the circle. These guidelines allow for almost any person of any birding level or age to participate. Money may be raised for a bird conservation project, but the main idea is to have a friendly competition with other birders.

There are many types of birding competitions and many ways birdwatchers compete with each other. Birders will compete to see who has more birds on their life list. They will also start competitions focused on finding the number of birds seen in a backyard, city, state, or year. Extreme birding takes on many different meanings depending on the birder. The fun thing about birding competitions is that it is up to the birder to decide what is extreme.

TAKING PHOTOGRAPHS

OR SKETCHING BIRDS IS A GOOD WAY TO REMEMBER THE ONES YOU ARE LEARNING TO IDENTIFY.

PART III

THE NEXT STEPS

CHAPTER NINE

BIRDING WITH A PURPOSE AND SAVING BIRDS

WORKING WITH OR SUPPORTING ORGANIZATIONS INVOLVED IN BIRD CONSERVATION

- *Saving birds*

- *Helping researchers and scientists*

- *Projects that make a difference*

- *Human hazards and how you can help*

There are many great organizations that make a difference in the lives of birds—too many to write about in this chapter. The organizations and their programs highlighted below make an effort to involve people in bird education and in bird conservation. Many of them believe that in order for people to understand why birds need to be conserved, they must first learn and understand more about birds and their needs. There is a great need for volunteers to put their time and talent into supporting the organizations and programs that help save birds. I hope you find one or more organizations to support or programs to help by volunteering. You will be well-rewarded knowing that future generations can enjoy a world that includes birds.

SAVING BIRDS

Many organizations work in collaboration to help save birds. Some of these alliances and partnerships are ongoing and some operate on an as-needed basis.

Bird Conservation Alliance (BCA—www. birdconservationalliance.org) is an alliance of non-profit organizations that have some focus on birds. This includes education, conservation, research, study, or the watching of birds. The Alliance is facilitated by the American Bird Conservancy (ABC), which conducts regular informational meetings, communicates to member organizations and agencies concerning bird conservation issues, and is an advocate for the protection of birds.

Partners in Flight (PIF—www.partnersinflight.org) is a cooperative effort involving partnerships among federal, state and local government agencies, professional organizations, conservation organizations, businesses, the academic community, and private individuals. Partners in Flight was launched in 1990 in response to growing concerns about declines in the populations of many land bird species. The initial focus was on neotropical migrants, species that breed in North America and winter in the Neotropics (Central and South America), but the focus has spread to include most land birds and other species requiring terrestrial habitats. The central premise of PIF has been that the resources of public and private organizations in North and South America need to be coordinated, with information and resource sharing increased in order to successfully conserve bird populations in the Western Hemisphere.

Organizations That Save Birds from Collisions

Ornithologists estimate that as many as one billion birds are killed every year in North America due to collisions with glass. Confused by artificial lights, blinded by weather, and unable to see glass, migratory birds by the hundreds and the thousands can be injured or killed colliding into one building in one night. Birds also fly into the glass windows of homes and businesses during daylight hours. Research findings by Daniel Klem, Ph.D., ornithologist and Professor of Biology at Muhlenberg College, and others, state that birds fly into windows because they cannot see glass.

Many ornithologists and conservationists believe the global problem of birds and collisions with glass may be the cause of decline for many bird species, some of which are already threatened with extinction. Many across the globe are working to address

ROYAL TERNS ARE COMMON ALONG THE GULF COAST AND SOUTHERN ATLANTIC COAST, FEEDING ON FISH AND CRABS.

this issue. The lights out efforts in Toronto, New York, Chicago, and other cities have a proven track record of saving birds. Several organizations such as the Fatal Light Awareness Program (FLAP) are members of the Bird Conservation Alliance (BCA) and have created programs and opportunities to reduce the impact of lighted buildings and to make buildings and glass safer for birds.

The Fatal Light Awareness Program (FLAP— www.flap.org/) works to educate office building managers in many cities. During migration, the Toronto skyline is darker because over 80 buildings have agreed to participate in the Bird-Friendly Building Program, launched by FLAP and World Wildlife Fund Canada. These buildings have earned the right to display the official Bird-Friendly Building logo. In January 2006 the Toronto City Council unanimously adopted a resolution that will protect migratory birds by controlling light from buildings. This resolution includes public education and bird rescue. Volunteers are needed to collect birds that do hit the buildings during their migration.

The Bird Conservation Network (BCN—www. bcnbirds.org) based in the Chicago, Illinois area works to promote and provide educational information to its coalition members about the Lights Out Chicago program. The Birds & Buildings Forum project is working to educate members of the building industry about preventing collisions in buildings and homes. Volunteers are always needed to spread the word.

MANY RESPECTED ORGANIZATIONS MAKE A DIFFERENCE IN THE CONSERVATION OF THE BIRDS WE ALL LOVE AND WATCH.

ONE OF THE SMALLEST HERONS IN THE WORLD, THE LEAST BITTERN CLINGS TO THE STEMS OF CATTAILS AND REEDS AS IT HUNTS FOR PREY.

that will produce a long-term solution to a major threat to migratory birds.

Out of this group, the Bird-Safe Glass Foundation was formed, which fund-raises to create educational materials for builders and consumers about birds and glass. Because the need to prevent collisions with glass is so urgent, NYC Audubon worked with the Bird-Safe Glass Working Group and the Bird-Safe Glass Foundation to publish a document called Bird-Safe Building Guidelines. This document is geared toward new building construction as well as retrofitting old buildings to be bird safe. It is available on the NYC Audubon website as a PDF.

Saving Cranes and Their Habitats

The International Crane Foundation (ICF—www.savingcranes.org/species/whooping.cfm) works worldwide to conserve cranes and the wetland and grassland ecosystems on which they depend. The ICF is recognized as the world center for the preservation of cranes. They are concerned with ecosystem protection and restoration and strive to alert scientists, government officials, and the public to the cranes' dependence on these habitats. You can support them by serving as a volunteer naturalist. ICF believes education is the key to protecting cranes and other wildlife and, through their volunteers, hope to reach a wide audience of future crane activists. ICF staff can also use volunteers with the daily routine of tending to the captive crane flock. The ICF also participates in the re-introduction of the whooping cranes in North America.

New York Audubon Society (NYC Audubon—www.nycaudubon.org) has shown great success with the Project Safe Flights Lights Out NY initiative, This encourages building owners and managers to turn off the lights at tall buildings to save the lives of night-migrating birds while reducing energy costs. Project Safe Flight convened the first Bird-Safe Glass Working Group (BSGWG), a multi-city task force charged with the goal of creating and promoting the development and use of a new type of glass that will be transparent to people but visible to birds. Using such glass on building exteriors could dramatically reduce the number of collisions. The group includes bird advocacy and conservation organizations from across North America, as well as architects, planners, scientists, and glass artists working to find funding for the cutting-edge science

Saving Migratory Birds

The Smithsonian Migratory Bird Center (http://nationalzoo.si.edu/ConservationAndScience/MigratoryBirds) is an organization dedicated to fostering greater understanding, appreciation, and protection of the grand phenomenon of bird migration. Smithsonian ornithologists have studied the impact of urbanization on birds, the conservation value of shade-grown coffee, the effect of global climate change on migratory birds, and the problem of emerging infectious diseases in birds.

American Bird Conservancy (ABC—www.abcbirds.org) works with coalitions of conservation groups, scientists, and the public to tackle conservation priorities to save wild birds and their habitats. Much of their work is focused on migratory birds, and ABC initiates, encourages, and leads collaborative programs while establishing consensus with other organizations using the best available science. ABC's International Program builds stronger partnerships and networks between North American, Latin American, and Caribbean organizations for better bird conservation. ABC has a long list of current conservation projects that are making a difference for migratory birds and all wild birds.

The United States Fish and Wildlife Service (USFWS—www.fws.gov/birds) is the principal federal agency charged with protecting and enhancing the populations and habitat of more than 800 species of birds that spend all or part of their lives in the United States. They support partnerships that deliver national and international management plans which conserve habitat for migratory birds and other wildlife. They offer grant programs to support and help organizations do conservation work. Most notable is the Neotropical Migratory Bird Conservation Act of 2000. This established a competitive, matching grants program supporting public–private partnerships in the United States, Canada, Latin America, and the Caribbean promoting the long-term conservation of neotropical migratory birds and their habitats. The goals include perpetuating healthy populations of neotropical migratory birds, providing financial resources for bird conservation initiatives, and fostering international cooperation for such initiatives.

THE YELLOW-BILLED MAGPIE IS FOUND IN CENTRAL CALIFORNIA. THEY CAN BE SEEN STEALING FOOD AT REST STOPS ALONG HIGHWAY 101.

FORAGING MOSTLY BELOW THE
SURFACE, THE RUDDY DUCK RARELY
LEAVES THE WATER.

Saving Ducks and Other Waterfowl

Ducks Unlimited (DU—www.ducks.org) is the leading waterfowl and wetlands conservation organization in North America. Because wetlands are critical to waterfowl and other wildlife species, DU has the single purpose of working to restore grassland, replant forests, restore watersheds, and work with landowners to establish conservation easements and management agreements. They work with many partners to accomplish their conservation work.

HELPING RESEARCHERS AND SCIENTISTS

Citizen science projects are a great way to get involved and to learn more about birds. Volunteers gather important information about birds that helps scientists make informed decisions about their management in national wildlife refuges, national parks, national forests, and other areas. The gathering of data through citizen science is an invaluable service to the birds and to the scientists that study them. Many of the projects listed below do not require special skills or experience.

Be aware that birds are protected by federal, state or provincial, and city or town laws. All native birds—belonging in the area naturally and not unlawfully introduced—are protected by federal laws. Anyone wanting to handle wild, native birds or to collect birds for any reason has to have a special permit. Rehabilitators need special permits. Even nature centers or educators who want to keep birds as part of their educational programs have to have special permits. All parts of birds are protected, including their feathers, eggs, and nests. Exceptions to federal laws include non-native species such as pigeons and English house sparrows, and hunting regulated species which have specific hunting seasons. Federal laws require permits for persons wanting to hunt birds. These permits have specific guidelines about what birds can be hunted, when, how many, and what sex in a season.

Listed below are projects for many levels of birders. Getting your family involved with some of the projects is a great way of sharing the joy of birds with them. I have also included information about the project sponsor organization(s) and contacts for further information.

Great Backyard Bird Count (GBBC—www. birdsource.org/gbbc) is a four-day count that occurs each year on the third weekend in February. This count is a joint project between the National Audubon Society and

ORVIS CONSERVATION EFFORTS

Many companies spend a considerable about of time and money supporting conservation and key projects and causes that benefit birds. One such company is Orvis. So far, their support and funding has assisted the endangered whooping crane, stream restoration in southern Vermont and New York, the McCloud River redband trout, and much more.

After being nearly extinct with fewer than 20 individuals in the wild, the beautiful whooping crane is making a comeback. There are now over 200 cranes thanks to the concentrated efforts of the International Crane Foundation, and the support of Orvis. Other successful birding initiatives include partnering with The Nature Conservancy to help protect critical habitat for the long billed curlew and the reestablishment of nest-ing colonies for the roseate tern. Orvis is also helping to protect a diverse range of habitats nationwide which are used by a variety of birds during their migratory cycles.

With its Round Up for Conservation initiatives and numerous other programs, The Orvis Company is committed to finding creative ways to fund worthy conservation efforts. Each year the company chooses three programs and matches customer donations through appeals in its mail order catalogs. The Orvis commitment to philanthropic efforts has resulted in the company donating more than ten million dollars over its history to advance environmental and humanitarian causes. For more information about Orvis and the conservation programs they support visit www.orvisconservation.com.

the Cornell Lab of Ornithology. Individuals, families, and community groups can participate in the GBBC by tracking the birds they see at their feeders and in their backyards, local parks, and other outdoor locations. GBBC information helps define bird ranges, populations, migration pathways, and habitat needs. This information has the potential to help with bird conservation issues. Participants count birds for as little or as long as they wish on one, two, three, or all four days. They tally the highest number of birds of each species seen together at any one time.

Project FeederWatch (www.birds.cornell.edu/pfw/) relies on volunteers to count

THE BIRD HOUSE NETWORK IS A CITIZEN SCIENCE PROJECT WHICH HELPS SCIENTISTS GATHER DATA ABOUT CAVITY-NESTING BIRDS.

birds that visit feeders at backyards, nature centers, community areas, and other locations in North America once every two weeks from November to April. The information helps scientists track broad-scale movements of birds in winter and long-term trends in bird distribution and abundance. Knowing the trends of feeder birds can help when scientists are considering the issues that face these backyard birds. Project FeederWatch is operated by the Cornell Lab of Ornithology and Bird Studies Canada. There is a $15 annual participation fee that covers materials, staff support, web design, data analysis, and a year-end report, called *Winter Bird Highlights*. This project is a great way to learn more about your backyard feeder birds and to share the experience with your family.

House Finch Disease Survey (http://www.birds.cornell.edu/hofi/) is a necessary and relatively easy survey where participants record the visits of house finches and American goldfinches at feeders and the occurrence of diseased birds. They send their data to the Cornell Lab of Ornithology. This helps scientists document the spread of mycoplasmal conjunctivitis in the United States and Canada. Typically, people who participate in Project FeederWatch also participate in this survey.

Project PredatorWatch (www.abcbirds.org/cats/) is initiated by the American Bird Conservancy to determine the extent of predation on birds at bird feeders and in people's backyards. Volunteers are critical in determining how many and what types of birds are killed by cats, dogs, hawks, and other predators. This information may help scientists understand the predator impacts on backyard birds.

The Birdhouse Network (www.birds.cornell.edu/birdhouse) asks volunteers to monitor North American cavity-nesting birds and their houses on a weekly basis. The Cornell Lab of Ornithology website offers guidelines and resources for the observer on how and when to monitor and other useful tips, including identifying nests and eggs. Observations are recorded on worksheets provided by the Cornell Lab, including date, nest box ID, nesting material, species, number of eggs, egg color, number of chicks, and so on. The data can be submitted online. This is a great way to learn more about cavity-nesting birds and get a personal look at the lives of the birds that nest in your area.

Christmas Bird Count (CBC—www.audubon.org/bird/cbc/) is a one-day annual event between December 14 and January 5. The primary objective of the CBC is to monitor the status and distribution of bird populations across the Western Hemisphere. Groups of volunteer birders count birds within a 15-mile (24 km) diameter circle. The CBC includes more than 2,000 circles each year, mostly in the United States and

FAMILY MEMBERS CAN PARTICIPATE IN THEIR LOCAL GREAT BACKYARD BIRD COUNT.

Canada. Its database now contains more than a century of data on early-winter bird populations across the Americas. Many studies have used CBC data. To determine population trends and dynamics of North American birds over the past 40 years, CBC data is combined with data from the Breeding Bird Survey. These studies help scientists see a clearer picture of how the continent's bird populations have changed over the past hundred years. Local trends in bird populations can indicate habitat fragmentation or signal an immediate environmental threat.

Other Citizen Science Projects

Many states have organizations or agencies that manage citizen science projects of some sort. Some of these projects are for monitoring breeding or non-migratory birds at a local level as well as keeping track of birds that may migrate through the area. Contact local organizations and agencies to see if there are projects or programs that may interest you. The following projects require some training or a more advanced skill level; some organizations may be willing to teach.

The Breeding Bird Survey (BBS-http://www.mp2-pwrc.usgs.gov/bbs/) requires a keen eye and a good knowledge of bird songs and calls. More than 3,000 Breeding Bird Survey routes are run along roadsides from May through June by experienced observers. This survey has been the foundation for many conservation plans and programs. The BBS is coordinated by the U.S. Geological Survey at Patuxent Wildlife Research Center in Maryland.

Birds in Forested Landscapes (BFL-www.birds.cornell.edu/) is a continent-wide study coordinated by Cornell Lab of Ornithology to look at the effects of habitat—especially for-est fragmentation—on the breeding success of thrushes and hawks. BFL focuses on seven species of North American thrushes—wood thrush, veery, Swainson's thrush, gray-cheeked thrush, varied thrush, hermit thrush, and Bicknell's thrush—and two forest raptors: Cooper's hawk and sharp-shinned hawk.

Golden-winged Warbler Atlas Project (www.birds.cornell.edu/gowap/birds.html) determines the population, habitat, and area requirements of golden-winged and blue-winged warblers and their hybrids. The golden-winged warbler is a neotropical migratory species of high conservation concern within Partners in Flight (PIF).

International Shorebird Survey (http://www.pwrc.usgs.gov/iss/iss.html) is coordinated by the Manomet Center for Conservation Sciences. Experienced volunteers east of the Rocky Mountains have counted shorebirds for the past twenty-five years. If you are particularly fond of shorebirds, especially during migration, this may be something you would like to do.

Bird-banding—Banding and catching birds require special permits. There are a variety of bird-banding activities that could be appropriate for a

CAPTURING AND BANDING BIRDS HELPS SCIENTISTS UNDERSTAND WHERE THEY TRAVEL.

beginning birder. Contact your local nature center or bird club to find a bird banding project near you.

Breeding Bird Atlases—Many states have done Breeding Bird Atlases by dividing the state into a grid system, then asking volunteers to determine the breeding status of all bird species within each square or a sample of the available squares. Contact your local bird club for more information.

PROJECTS THAT MAKE A DIFFERENCE
Helping Latin American Countries Research and Conserve Birds

Birders' Exchange (www.americanbirding. org/bex/index.html). Now run by the American Birding Association, Birder's Exchange was originally founded in 1990 by the Manomet Center for Conservation Science (MCCS). Because many researchers, educators, and conservationists in Latin American countries work without some of the basic equipment, Birders' Exchange provides new and used equipment to them. Since its inception, Birders' Exchange has served more than 500 groups in 30 countries and territories.

Birders' Exchange needs volunteer couriers to deliver equipment. If you are planning to take a trip to a country in Latin America or to the Caribbean, you could volunteer to take donated equipment in your luggage on behalf of Birders' Exchange. They try to arrange airport meetings with the organizations in need, but you may be asked

BECOMING INVOLVED WITH CITIZEN SCIENCE PROJECTS IS A GOOD WAY TO LEARN MORE ABOUT BIRDS AND CONTRIBUTE TO THEIR CONSERVATION.

POPULATIONS OF THE THE PURPLE FINCH HAVE DECLINED, IN PART DUE TO COMPETITION FROM HOUSE SPARROWS AND HOUSE FINCHES.

http://www.americanbird-ing.org/bex/index.html
bpetersen@aba.org

Keeping Cats Indoors and Saving Birds

The American Bird Conservancy (ABC) launched Cats Indoors! a Campaign for Safer Birds and Cats to educate cat owners, decision-makers, and the general public that everybody benefits when cats are kept indoors. No one knows exactly how many birds are killed by cats every year, although nationwide, cats are estimated to kill hundreds of millions of birds and more than a billion small mammals, such as rabbits, chipmunks, squirrels, and shrews each year. Cats also kill rare and endangered species for which the loss of even one animal is significant. In the United States, these endangered species include the piping plover, California least tern, and San Clemente loggerhead shrike. Cats also kill small native mammals key to maintaining ecosystems and acting as vital food sources for raptors such as great horned owls, red-tailed hawks, and American kestrels.

There are over 73 million pet cats in the United States. A recent poll shows approximately 35 percent are kept exclusively indoors, leaving more than 40 million free to kill birds and other wildlife. In addition, millions of stray and feral cats roam our cities, suburbs, farmlands, and natural areas. These cats are victims of human irresponsibility through

to visit the exact location of the project. They try to work out the best arrangement for you, and for the project. You need to contact Birders' Exchange well in advance of your trip so the organization can send equipment and prepare all documentation needed for customs. If you aren't planning a trip and can't serve as a courier, there are other ways you can help. You can make a donation of new or used equipment or make a financial donation to purchase specialized equipment and books, and to cover shipping costs. You can also offer to show a seven minute Birders' Exchange video at your garden club, bird club, local business, school, or church group.

For more information contact:
Betty Petersen, Birders' Exchange
Program Director
American Birding Association
4945 N 30th St, Suite 200
Colorado Springs, CO 80919

owner abandonment and the failure to spay or neuter pets. Estimates for homeless cats range from 60 to 100 million. These creatures lead short, miserable lives. Outdoor cats on average live three to five years. Indoor cats commonly live 17 years. Free-roaming cats can also spread disease to humans and other animals. Keeping pets indoors benefits everyone.

ABC developed many education materials, including fact sheets, posters, the brochure, "Keeping Cats Indoors Isn't Just for the Birds, an Educator's Guide for Grades K-6," as well as print and radio public service announcements. Many organizations, including the New Jersey Audubon Society, have joined ABC in developing programs to educate people about keeping their cats indoors.

For more information contact:
Cats Indoors! Campaign
American Bird Conservancy
1731 Connecticut Ave., NW, 3rd Fl
Washington, DC 20009
202-234-7181
www.abcbirds.org/cats/

Reintroducing Endangered Whooping Cranes

Whooping cranes are endangered, and their numbers greatly declined due to hunting, drainage of wetlands, and conversion of grasslands to agriculture. Only fifteen or sixteen cranes survived the winter of 1941–42. The present world population is less than 500 wild and captive whooping cranes. Only one self-sustaining population survives in the wild. Migrating 2,500 miles (4,000 km) twice annually these wild cranes winter at the Aransas National Wildlife Refuge on the Gulf of Mexico and nest in Wood Buffalo National Park in Canada. Whooping cranes, like all cranes and geese, learn to migrate by following their parents. This knowledge is lost if there are no parents to show the way.

Fortunately, inventor and artist Bill Lishman came up with a solution. In 1993, Lishman and fellow artist-turned-biologist, Joe Duff, used ultralight aircraft to lead a small flock of Canada Geese from Ontario, Canada to Virginia, USA. The unassisted return migration of this flock of geese the following spring gained worldwide attention and led to the making of the film *Fly Away Home*, by Columbia Pictures. This method of teaching migration to captive-reared birds is used to reintroduce endangered whooping cranes in the wild.

LOCAL RESCUE OPERATIONS INCLUDE FEEDING INJURED ANIMALS SUCH AS BIRD HAWKS.

The Operation Migration team in partnership with the Whooping Crane Eastern Partnership works to reintroduce endangered whooping cranes into the eastern part of North America. In the first five years of the program, approximately 60 whooping cranes have been taught a migration route between Wisconsin and Florida. This is four times the number that existed in the early 1940s. Visit www.bringbackthecranes.org/index.html for more information about the reintroduction efforts for the whooping crane, and visit www.operationmigration.org for more information about Operation Migration. The Orvis company has been a generous supporter and contributor to Operation Migration.

People and Parrots

The People and Parrots Project, a partnership between the Bahamas National Trust and the University of Florida, aims to increase awareness about Abaco National Park in the Bahamas and its endangered Bahama parrot. Abaco National Park was established primarily to protect the habitat and breeding range of the Bahama parrot and its rapidly diminishing Caribbean pine forest habitat. The park is believed to support a third of the surviving Bahama parrot population. Today the parrots number less than 3,000, found only on Abaco and Great Inagua islands.

Abaco National Park offers opportunities for both locals and tourists to hike, birdwatch, cave, explore, and enjoy nature in a unique environment. Seven groups from different communities in Abaco agreed that the top benefit offered by Abaco National Park was the protection of the Bahama parrot. The second most important benefit was its potential for education, targeting schoolchildren, the general public, and tourists. The group also agreed that parrot protection should preclude recreation opportunities when and where the two are in conflict.

Several strategies were developed to avoid the issue of human–parrot conflict. One way was to establish parrot protection zones where humans are limited or excluded, especially during the parrot breeding season. The project also continues to monitor the health of the Bahama parrot as well as other wildlife and ecological systems in the park. They provide local guides with extensive knowledge of the park to lead visitors through sensitive areas.

Abaco National Park is considered a valuable educational opportunity for both residents of Abaco and tourists to learn about the natural and cultural environment of the area. The Trust's Education Office produced many educational brochures and a Pine Forest Teachers Resource Kit. The project was so successful in meeting its first-year objectives that a second year of funding has been granted to the project by the Disney Foundation. The key to success has been involving the local community, and the great support of organizations such as the Friends of the Environment and the Bahamas Ministry of Tourism. For more information, visit www.thebahamasnationaltrust.org/partners.php.

Important Bird Areas

Several organizations have Important Bird Areas (IBA) Programs. The goal of the IBA Program is not just to recognize sites as important, but to mobilize the resources needed to protect the sites for birds and other wildlife. The selection of Important Bird Areas has been an effective way to identify conservation priorities. Many are small enough to be conserved in their entirety, and many are often already part of a protected area. The IBA designation raises awareness of the importance of each site and its value to bird conservation among the public and land managers. Despite the fact that most IBAs are on protected land, there are many threats such as introduced species, soil erosion, sub-

urban sprawl, overuse for recreation, lack of funding for management and infrastructure, groundwater insufficiency, water diversion or drainage, excessive disturbance, overgrazing, pollution, pesticides, and fire.

The American Bird Conservancy's Important Bird Areas Program was launched in 1995 and has concentrated on identifying and documenting the most important sites throughout the United States. Many kinds of sites are represented: national wildlife refuges, national parks and forests, state lands, conservation organization lands, and some private lands. Some of these sites are important because they are links along a migratory pathway. A few, most notably several in Hawaii, support species found

THE PEREGRINE FALCON CAN DIVE TO CAPTURE PREY AT SPEEDS WELL OVER 100 MILES (160.9 KM) PER HOUR.

nowhere else on earth. Using objective scientific information and relying on the recommendations of experts throughout the United States, ABC has developed a list and set of descriptions of 500 of these internationally significant sites.

The IBA Program of BirdLife International aims to identify, monitor, and protect a global network of IBAs for the conservation of the world's birds and other biodiversity. BirdLife Partners take responsibility for the IBA Program nationally. The National Audubon Society runs the program in the United States. Canada's Important Bird Areas Program is a partnership between Bird Studies Canada, Nature Canada, and BirdLife International. It is a science-based initiative designed to identify, conserve, and monitor a network of sites. These sites provide essential habitat for Canada's bird populations. Since IBAs are monitored by national and local organizations as well as individuals working on the ground, the IBA Program can be a powerful way to build national institutional capacity and establish an effective conservation program to protect the areas important for birds. As of 2004, BirdLife International has identified over 7,500 sites in almost 170 countries as Important Bird Areas.

For more information about the Important Bird Areas Programs visit: American Bird Conservancy at www.abcbirds.org/iba/; BirdLife International (www.birdlife.org/action/science/sites/index.html); Canada IBA (www.ibacanada.com); or the National Audubon Society (www.audubon.org/bird/iba/index.html).

Park Flight and Migratory Birds
The Park Flight Migratory Bird Program works to protect migratory bird species and their habitats in both United States and Latin American national parks and protected areas. The program develops bird conservation and education projects and creates opportunities for technical exchange and cooperation. The United States National Park System provides critical habitat for many species of migratory birds, from raptors and shorebirds to songbirds. These species use parks on a seasonal basis and their protection cannot be assured without con-

THE WILSON'S PLOVER MIGRATES TO THE SOUTHERN GULF COAST AND SOUTH AMERICA. IT HAS A LONGER AND THICKER BILL THAN MOST PLOVERS, GIVING IT A WIDER RANGE OF FEEDING OPTIONS.

servation efforts occurring in the habitats the birds use throughout the year.

Park Flight coordinates programs between the United States and Latin America to protect breeding, migration, and wintering habitats. It is a partnership between the National Park Service, the National Park Foundation, and National Fish & Wildlife Foundation. For more information visit www.nps.gov/oia/topics/flight.htm.

SHADE-GROWN COFFEE PROVIDES HABITAT FOR BIRDS IN CENTRAL AND SOUTH AMERICA.

Coffee and Saving Habitats for Birds

Many people don't realize that coffee is sometimes grown in sunny plantations and sometimes in the shade, and that constitutes a huge difference in the lives of birds. Producing coffee using shade-grown production methods, in contrast to sun-grown coffee, provides food and shelter for songbirds as well as habitat for many other species of animals and plants. Unfortunately, many farmers have been encouraged to convert their practices to sun-grown systems because more bushes can be cultivated per acre. Each plant produces three times more coffee than a shade bush in a given year.

While sun-grown coffee produces increased yields, it requires the addition of chemical fertilizers, insecticides, herbicides, and fungicides. Because the land is cleared to allow the sun to reach the coffee plants,

the lack of tree root structures in the soil causes increased erosion and toxic run-off. The tree canopy in shade coffee plantations protect the soil from erosion and provide natural mulch for coffee plants, reducing the need for chemical fertilizers and herbicides.

In the mid-elevations of Mexico, Central America, the Caribbean, and Colombia, most of the forests still standing are in traditional coffee plantations. These provide the last refuge for birds that have lost their habitat to the vast destruction of tropical forests. Swallows, warblers, orioles, tanagers, and other native and migratory birds find a safe haven in these remaining forests. Scientists and birdwatchers have noticed a marked decline in migratory bird populations over the last twenty-five years.

Several independent, nonprofit organizations have developed standards to certify coffee as "shade-grown," "organic," and/or "fair trade." However, standards vary from organization to organization, and certification is not always achievable for all shade-grown coffee. Many farmers, importers, roasters, and retailers are committed to providing shade-grown coffee but cannot meet the rigor of various forms of third-party certification. A number of organizations sell shade-grown coffee, and they often contribute to bird conservation through their coffee sales. For more information, see: American Birding Association (www.americanbirding. org/resources/shadecoffee/songbird.html), American Bird Conservancy (www.abcbirds. org), National Audubon Society (www. auduboncoffeeclub.com/shop/home.php), Seattle Audubon/Northwest Shade Coffee (http://www.shadecoffee.org), Smithsonian Migratory Bird Center (http://nationalzoo. si.edu/ConservationandScience/MigratoryBirds/Coffee).

HUMAN HAZARDS AND HOW YOU CAN HELP

Birds thrill, enchant, and amaze us. Think about the everyday life of a bird. To survive, they have to find food, water, and places to raise their young and shelter them from the elements. Think about the hazards they face, both in nature and from humans. The most common hazards include flying into windows, communication towers, and power lines. The leading causes of declining bird populations are loss and fragmentation of habitat. These result from development, road construction, intensive agriculture, and other land uses.

In addition to these well-known hazards, commercial and residential pesticide use and longline fishing practices harm birds as well. While there is no one centralized database that collects all the information on bird kills, there are about 200 databases and research accountings with varying levels of information. Their findings, while valuable, probably provide only a glimpse of the total number of actual bird kills. There are things you can do in your own backyard to help birds. The next time you are asked by an organization to sign a petition or call your local representative supporting policy changes that protect birds, consider supporting their efforts. Below are some issues that have major impacts on bird populations, and

THE LITTLE BLUE HERON FEEDS IN MARSHES, SWAMPS, PONDS, AND RICE FIELDS. ITS DIET CONSISTS OF MOSTLY FISH AND CRUSTACEANS.

some of the organizations that are working on the issues in an effort to make changes for the better.

Pesticide Use

Some pesticides can, and do, kill songbirds, gamebirds, raptors, sea and shorebirds, and more. The United States Environmental Protection Agency (USEPA) has documented over 1100 incidents of bird kills—including hundreds of individual birds—attributable to pesticide use. Pesticides can kill birds both directly and indirectly. On farms alone, 672 million birds are directly exposed each year to pesticides, according to one conservative estimate, and 10 percent of these, or roughly 67 million birds, die. According to the United States Fish & Wildlife Service, approximately 50 pesticides currently used in the United States have caused bird die-offs.

Although DDT is banned in the United States, it is still widely used in other countries and continues to affect neotropical migratory bird species adversely. They maintain high levels of DDT in their fat, and during times of stress, birds metabolize the fat, releasing toxins into their blood, causing effects such as eggshell thinning. Several organizations are working together through the National Pesticide Reform Coalition to understand the impact pesticides have on birds and what can be done to reduce deaths due to pesticide poisoning.

This coalition initiated by the American Bird Conservancy includes many national organizations. The Avian Incident Monitor-

BE CAREFUL WITH PESTICIDE USE. MANY CAN SERIOUSLY HARM OR KILL BIRDS.

ing System (AIMS), a program dedicated to improving identification, investigation, and laboratory analysis of pesticide poisoned birds, is a cooperative program between American Bird Conservancy (ABC) and the United States Environmental Protection Agency (USEPA). Through AIMS, ABC is implementing programs that the National Pesticide Reform Coalition can use as they try to work together to protect birds from pesticides. For more information about the pesticide issue, contact www.abcbirds.org, and for information about the AIMS database, please visit (www.abcbirds.org/aims).

Longline Fishing

Longline fishing uses 35,000 baited hooks on lines that may extend for 60 miles (97 km) in the ocean. These lines are baited with whole fish or squid and are deployed by freezer autoliner vessels. While the lines are being set, seabirds dive at the bait, and

LONGLINE FISHING AND LEAD POISONING
FROM LEAD SINKERS KILL HUNDREDS OF
THOUSANDS OF SEA AND SHORE BIRDS
EACH YEAR.

have gone up since 1997 regulations were adopted, indicating that the regulations have not been effective in reducing the problem. Several key organizations are working to reduce seabird mortality in longline fisheries. Visit American Bird Conservancy (www.abcbirds.org) or BirdLife International (www.birdlife.org) and Blue Ocean (www.blueocean.org) to learn more about saving seabirds.

Lead Sinkers

What does fishing and lead tackle have to do with birds? Every year loons and other waterbirds die from lead poisoning due to the ingestion of lead tackle, especially lead sinkers. When lead fishing sinkers are lost through broken line or dropped in the water, birds can inadvertently eat them. Birds like loons and swans can swallow lead when they scoop up pebbles from the bottom of a lake or river to help grind their food.

Eagles, ospreys, and other birds ingest lead by eating fish which have swallowed sinkers.

Ingestion of lead sinkers is toxic enough to cause death by acute lead poisoning in many birds, and causes adverse effects on the nervous and reproductive systems of birds. A bird with lead poisoning can have physical and behavioral changes, including loss of balance, tremors, and an impaired ability to fly or find food properly. The weakened bird is more vulnerable to predators. It may also have trouble caring for its young. It becomes

can become impaled on the hooks. They are pulled down into the water and eventually drown. Seabirds can also swallow baited hooks during line retrieval.

Each year, hundreds of thousands of seabirds die from longliners worldwide, and longline fisheries have significantly increased throughout the world's oceans. From 1997 through 1999, longline vessels in Alaska killed an average of 20,341 seabirds per year, including 2,425 black-footed albatrosses, and from 1993 through 1999, 6,721 Laysan albatrosses were killed in the Alaskan longline fishery. Thirteen endangered short-tailed albatrosses were killed from 1996 to 1999. Seabird mortality rates in the key Alaskan fishery area weak and emaciated and often dies within two to three weeks after eating the lead.

Lead is found in most fishing jigs and sinkers, however, there are alternatives to traditional lead tackle. Ten years ago, Orvis was the first company to remove lead from all their weighted sinkers. Anglers can now use sinkers and jigs made from non-poisonous materials such as tin, bismuth, steel, and tungsten-nickel alloy, which can be found at established sporting goods retailers such as Orvis (www.orvis.com).

Communication Towers

The US Fish & Wildlife Service (USFWS) estimates at least five million birds and as many as 50 million birds are killed annually in collisions with communications towers in the United States. There are more than 85,000 towers providing coverage for television, radio, cell phones, and other industries. More than 60,000 of these towers are required by the Federal Communications Commission to be lighted, either because they are over 199 feet (60 m) tall, are in the immediate vicinity of an airport, or are situated along major highway travel routes.

Two hundred and thirty species of birds have been documented as being killed at towers, over one quarter of all avian species found in the United States. Most birds killed are neotropical migratory songbirds which migrate at night, and their navigation systems seem to be confused by the tower lights, particularly in bad weather. Further documents report that 52 of these 230 species killed at towers are on either the USFWS's

most recent Nongame Birds of Management Concern List or the Partners in Flight (PIF) Watch List. This means species killed at towers, including black rail, Bell's vireo, golden-winged warbler, Swainson's warbler, Henslow's sparrow, Bachman's sparrow, and McCown's longspur are in decline and in need of special management attention.

Towers kill many migratory birds and are another human threat to healthy populations of birds. Further research is being conducted to determine the exact cause of bird deaths at towers, and how lighting systems and other aspects of tower construction and operation may be modified to avoid such mortality. The American Bird Conservancy works with industries and organizations to find safe solutions. For more information about towers and birds visit www.abcbirds.org.

COLLISIONS WITH COMMUNICATIONS TOWERS ARE CAUSING THE DECLINE OF A NUMBER OF BIRD SPECIES.

CHAPTER TEN

ADDITIONAL RESOURCES

A LIST OF SUPPLEMENTARY
RESOURCES FOR BIRDERS

- *Organizations*

- *Publications*

- *Books*

- *Birding online*

There are many organizations that focus on birds. Some concentrate on the hobby of birdwatching and others on research. Many are connected with bird conservation. A number of the organizations listed below combine birdwatching, research, and conservation. Most have online educational materials and up-to-date information about issues that may negatively or positively impact birds. Many of them offer ways that you can participate in their work to help birds and their conservation. See Chapter Nine for more details.

Many birds-related organizations operate on very tight, nonprofit budgets and rely on memberships and grants to accomplish their goals. This is especially true of those that focus on research and conservation. They desperately need the support of birdwatchers. This can be in the form of an individual or family membership into the organization, or research and monitoring help with citizen science or conservation projects. Financial donations are always welcome.

I have listed the national, nonprofit organizations and government agencies I feel offer reliable information and services to people interested in watching birds. They also provide information about conservation and research. They are listed in alphabetical order and the description of each is taken mostly from their mission and goals statements, with some personal comments from me. If you are interested in a more comprehensive list of organizations that have an interest in birds, you can visit the Bird Conservation Alliance Website (www.birdconservationalliance.org) and click on their member list. You should also check for local bird club and resource information by contacting your local nature center, zoo, or natural history museum.

ORGANIZATIONS

American Bird Conservancy (ABC—www.abcbirds.org) The American Bird Conservancy is a nonprofit membership organization, whose mission is to conserve wild birds and their habitats throughout the Americas.

THE WESTERN SANDPIPER IS ONE OF THE MOST COMMON SHOREBIRDS IN NORTH AMERICA. IT IS OFTEN MISTAKEN FOR THE SLIGHTLY SMALLER SEMIPALMATED SANDPIPER.

It is the only U.S.-based group dedicated solely to overcoming the greatest threats facing birds in the Western Hemisphere. A growing human population consuming ever greater resources is critically impacting bird populations through habitat destruction, harmful practices like the unwise use of pesticides, and the introduction of destructive species including domestic cats. ABC believes adequate resources exist to overcome these threats, and that unifying people, organizations, and agencies is the key to success. ABC draws on people and organizations through bird conservation networks including the Bird Conservation Alliance, the North American Bird Conservation Initiative, Partners in Flight, and a growing international organization network, to identify the most critical issues affecting birds throughout the Americas.

American Birding Association (ABA—www.americanbirding.org) The ABA is a nonprofit organization that provides leadership to birders by increasing their knowledge, skills, and enjoyment of birding. They are the only organization in North America that specifically caters to recreational birders. The ABA represents a whole range of birding interests, from identification and education to listing and conservation. They actively promote the economic and environmental values of birding, and they encourage the conservation of birds and their habitats. They have a variety of programs. More information about their Birder's Exchange program is found in Chapter Nine.

Bird Studies Canada (BSC—www.bsc-eoc.org) Bird Studies Canada is a nonprofit membership organization committed to advancing the understanding, appreciation, and conservation of Canada's wild birds and their habitats. It conducts research throughout Canada through volunteer-based surveys such as the Canadian Lakes Loon Survey and Project FeederWatch. In addition, it coordinates the analysis of data collected by a growing network of observatories monitoring migratory birds across Canada through the Canadian Migration Monitoring Network.

Cornell Lab of Ornithology (CLO—www.birds.cornell.edu) The Cornell Lab of Ornithology is a nonprofit membership institution whose mission is to interpret and conserve the earth's biological diversity through research, education, and citizen science focused on birds. Their programs work with citizen scientists, governmental, and nongovernmental agencies across North America and beyond. They believe that bird enthusiasts of all ages and skill levels can and do make a difference. The CLO provides many resources and tools for birders, and has a great Home Study Course for birders. It is an excellent way to learn a lot about birds, their lives, and their behavior, and offers opportunities to participate in citizen

BIRDING RESOURCES

ARE READILY AVAILABLE TO HELP BEGINNERS LEARN MORE ABOUT BIRDS AND BIRD WATCHING.

DOUBLE-CRESTED CORMORANTS NEST IN TREES OR CLIFFS NEAR WATER, OR ON AN ISLAND.

a nonprofit membership institution with the mission to inspire Americans to protect wildlife for our children's future. The Federation's Garden for Wildlife program gives people a step-by-step process to certify their yards as Backyard Wildlife Habitats by providing the essential elements—food, water, shelter, and places to raise young. The Habitat Stewards program trains volunteers to run workshops to help people create Backyard Wildlife Habitats.

Nature Canada (NC—www.naturecanada. ca) Nature Canada is dedicated to fostering awareness and appreciation of the natural world. They are a member-based nonprofit conservation organization with a mission to protect nature, its diversity, and the processes that sustain it. They support on-the-ground, community-based efforts to protect animals, plants, and habitat; advocate for effective laws; and support policies that protect endangered species, conserve bird habitat, and promote biodiversity in Canada and abroad.

North American Bluebird Society (NABS—www.nabluebirdsociety.org) The goal of the North American Bluebird Society is to support research about and to promote the recovery of bluebirds and other native cavity-nesting birds. The society sponsors the Transcontinental Bluebird Trail, which includes more than 18,000 nesting boxes across North America. Bluebirds tend to nest in natural holes found in trees, and their numbers had been declining because of habitat loss. Creating manmade nesting boxes for bluebirds has helped their numbers increase.

science projects. More information about these projects is in Chapter Nine.

National Audubon Society (NAS—www.audubon.org) The National Audubon Society is a nonprofit membership organization whose mission is to conserve and restore natural ecosystems—focusing on birds, other wildlife, and their habitats—for the benefit of humanity and the earth's biological diversity. They are a national network of community-based nature centers and chapters with scientific, educational, and advocacy programs. They focus their work to benefit areas sustaining important bird populations.

National Wildlife Federation (NWF—www. nwf.org) The National Wildlife Federation is

Ornithological Council (OC—www.nmnh. si.edu/BIRDNET) The Ornithological Council, a public information organization, is supported by eleven North American professional ornithological societies. The BIRDNET website lists these societies and provides information about ornithology—the scientific study of birds. It links the scientific community with public and private decision-makers. The Council provides timely information about birds to ensure scientifically-based decisions, policies, and management actions. The Council also informs ornithologists of proposals and actions that affect birds or the study of birds and speaks for scientific ornithology on public issues.

Patuxent Wildlife Research Center (PWRC— www.pwrc.usgs.gov/birds) The Patuxent Wildlife Research Center has been a national and international leader in wildlife

LOCAL NEWSPAPERS OFTEN RUN ARTICLES ON BIRDWATCHING AND CONSERVATION.

NEWSPAPERS

Some newspapers publish regular columns specifically about birds and birdwatching and others will occasionally publish such articles. These articles are sometimes written by nationally-syndicated authors including David Sibley. These articles are popular because they focus on local birding and often engage local bird club members and naturalists, who then share the information with other birders. If your newspaper doesn't have a regular column about birds or birdwatching, consider suggesting to them that their readers would appreciate more stories on this subject.

TOP: THE SULAWESI TARICTIC HORNBILL IS ENDEMIC TO INDONESIA IN THE TROPICAL LOWLANDS AND SWAMPS. BOTTOM RIGHT: THE TOCO TOUCAN IS NOT A GREAT FLIER AND SPENDS MOST OF ITS TIME IN HOLLOW TREES. BOTTOM LEFT: THE VICTORIA CROWNED PIGEON, FOUND NEW GUINEA AND NEARBY ISLANDS, IS THE LARGEST PIGEON LIVING TODAY.

research since its creation by Congress in 1936 as an integral part of the Patuxent Research Refuge. Patuxent is one of seventeen Research Centers of the U.S. Geological Survey (USGS), the natural resources research arm of the Department of the Interior (DOI). In partnership with the Canadian Wildlife Service, Patuxent is nationally recognized as the U.S. Bird Banding Laboratory. It provides numbered leg bands to bird banders, and manages huge databases of bandings and recoveries essential for many migratory bird management and research applications. Patuxent offers many tools that help scientists and birdwatchers learn more about birds. These tools include: Patuxent's Bird ID InfoCenter, Patuxent Bird Quiz, Bird Identification Tips, and Seasonal Bird Checklists. The "Birds of North America" Usage Tool is a reference tool for a series of bird "biographies" published by The Birds of North America.

Smithsonian Migratory Bird Center (SMBC—www.nationalzoo.si.edu/ ConservationAndScience/MigratoryBirds) The Smithsonian Migratory Bird Center is dedicated to fostering greater understanding, appreciation, and protection of the grand phenomenon of bird migration. They clarify the causes for declines in migratory bird populations, raising awareness of migratory birds and the need to protect their habitats. The Center conducts a variety of outreach programs

and protects habitats that are crucial to the annual pilgrimage of migratory birds in the Western Hemisphere. The website offers a variety of webcams to view birds and has tools for educators. More information is available in Chapter Nine.

PUBLICATIONS

There are a great number of publications available to a person interested in birds and birdwatching. These publications vary from scientific journals and monthly or bimonthly magazines to newsletters and e-newsletters. Many are supported by the advertisements contained in the magazine or by organization memberships, and some organizations support their publications themselves.

THE RED-BREASTED NUTHATCH FEEDS ON SEEDS AND INSECTS FOUND ON TREE BARK. THEY HAVE AN EARLY MIGRATION CYCLE, WHICH CAN BEGIN IN JULY.

Magazines

Magazines and newsletters provide current news and information such as where and when to find birds, birding techniques, and who's who in the birding world. Most magazines contain wonderful photography and well-written articles about birdwatching or conservation issues. Magazines typically hire well-known and experienced birders to write many of the articles. It is clear when you read their publications that the editors are passionately devoted to birds. Subscribing to one or two birding magazines will keep you up-to-date with the world of birdwatching and other issues concerning birds.

Audubon Magazine is published by the National Audubon Society. Membership in

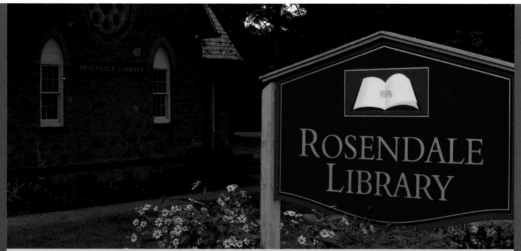

LIBRARIES OFFER A WIDE VARIETY OF RESOURCES ON BIRDING AND WILL ORDER BOOKS, VIDEOS, CDs, AND OTHER SOURCE MATERIAL IF REQUESTED.

PUBLIC LIBRARIES

Public libraries often have a great section on birds, birdwatching, and nature in general. Your library should have at least a few of the basic reference guides. You may occasionally need these guides, but they can take up too much space or be too costly for you to own. If you are in or near a large city, the main branch of the library may have a plethora of books, journals, and archived newspaper articles that may be of interest to you. Librarians are usually eager to answer your questions about birds. Don't forget about libraries in nature centers or zoos. While they may not let you take a book home, they will allow you to use it while you are there. What better place to read about birds while you are sitting at the nature center window watching them?

the organization includes the subscription to their bimonthly magazine. The magazine, while beautiful, contains a large amount of advertising and departs regularly from a main focus on birds.

For more information contact:

National Audubon Society
700 Broadway
New York, NY 10003
Phone: (212) 979-3000
https://websvr.audubon.org/forms/up-dated/new_order.html

Birding, the American Birding Association's 35-year-old, bimonthly flagship publication features broad coverage of various aspects of bird identification and bird finding. It includes ABA organization membership. The magazine also presents expert media reviews and features a photo quiz for its readers. This magazine is great for the serious and the beginning birder, and contains moderate advertising, mostly by tour companies and birding businesses.

For more information contact:

ABA Membership
4945 N 30th Street, Suite 200
Colorado Springs, CO 80919
(800) 850-2473 or (719) 578-9703
https://commerce10.pair.com/ambirder/memformR.htm

Bird Conservation quarterly magazine is available through a membership to American Bird Conservancy, keeping readers abreast of all the issues affecting wild birds in the United States, Canada, Latin America, and the Caribbean. The magazine also provides

the latest developments from Partners in Flight, the North American Bird Conservation Initiative (NABCI), habitat issues, and American Bird Conservancy programs. There are great photos and articles about birds of special concern, and no advertising.

For more information contact:

American Bird Conservancy
PO Box 249
The Plains, VA 20198
540-253-5780
www.abcbirds.org/membership

Bird Watcher's Digest is a commercial publication and packed with content, including tips and advice from experts. A lot of bird art and photographs accompany articles to help with identification and to add to your enjoyment of birdwatching. While it does contain advertising, it is mostly from tour companies and birding specialist companies. The magazine is owned by a birdwatching family who takes birds seriously while having fun.

For more information contact:

Bird Watcher's Digest
P.O. Box 110 (149 Acme Street)
Marietta, OH 45750
740-373-5285/1-800-879-2473
www.birdwatchersdigest.com/site/index.aspx

Birder's World is a commercial bimonthly publication full of wonderful photography and compelling articles on a wide range of topics. The magazine contains identification tips and unique issues about birds and birdwatching and is great for beginning and advanced birdwatchers. The magazine does contain advertising.

For more information contact:
Kalmbach Publishing Co.
21027 Crossroads Circle
P.O. Box 1612
Waukesha, WI 53187-1612
800-533-6644
www.birdersworld.com

Birds and Blooms is a fun and colorful magazine filled with stories about people and the birds they love. It is a bimonthly publication with a focus on gardening and backyard birds and butterflies.

For more information contact:
Reiman Publications
5400 South 60th Street
Greendale, Wisconsin 53129
800-344-6913
www.birdsandblooms.com

Wild Bird Magazine is a bimonthly commercial magazine that includes a variety of articles and lots of good photography. The magazine offers readers a chance to submit photos for a photo contest and keeps readers up-to-date with the fun side of birdwatching.

For more information contact:
Wild Bird Magazine/Corporate Address
P.O. Box 57900
Los Angeles, CA 90057
213-385-2222
www.wildbirdmagazine.com/wb

BOOKS

There are a huge number of books about birds and birdwatching. These include field guides, how-to books, bird finding guides, and books of essays about birding. As you start to buy books on birds and birding, you may find that your collection grows quickly and will also include other nature and natural history topics. The average bookstore may carry a basic supply of books and can order books if you know which ones you want. You may have good luck at a store specializing in bird-feeding and birdwatching products. The American Birding Association has a special sales division that just offers books, and this is where you can find many of the bird finding guides. Many nature centers, zoos, and museums have a nice selection of books as well. You can buy books online, though I find being able to see the book in person is very satisfying. Explore your options.

State and Local Guides

Many states have guides designed specifically to guide birdwatchers to various locations and habitats where birds can be found. The state guides typically detail habitats and the location and time of year when birds are most likely to be present. They are a great way to explore your state or a state you plan to visit. Most of these books are very accurate, but you could find a location has been closed or may be temporarily off-limits to birdwatchers.

Books on General Birdwatching

There are a number of good books to enhance your birdwatching hobby. Usually written by experienced birdwatchers, they can help you learn more about the identification of birds. Here are some choices:

Identify Yourself: 50 Common Bird ID Challenges by Bill Thompson III. A good book for the more advanced birdwatchers as well as for beginners, *Identify Yourself* goes into great detail to help birders distinguish between similar bird species. For example, you'll learn how to identify hawks and how to tell little brown sparrows apart. It examines groupings of bird species that are commonly encountered but difficult to identify and combines clear, easy-to-understand text with illustrations that show key field marks for easy visual comparison.

THE ROSE-BREASTED GROSBEAK IS A STRIKING BIRD THAT LIVES AND BREEDS MOSTLY IN DECIDUOUS FORESTS AND ORCHARDS.

Sibley's Birding Basics by David Allen Sibley includes sixteen short chapters that focus on getting started as a birder. It discusses challenges in bird identification, describes how birds are classified, and emphasizes the value of behavioral and habitat cues in birding. The book also explains the details of soft-part colors and how plumage varies with season, age, wear, and molt.

The Sibley Guide to Bird Life and Behavior by David Sibley is a must-have book. Here, Sibley goes beyond the identification of birds to detail how birds live and how they behave. He has the help of forty-eight other experts and biologists to provide an amazing amount of information that will only fuel your desire to view birds.

The Lives of North American Birds, the *Peterson Field Guide to Advanced Birding*, and *The Field Guide to Birds of North America*, by Kenn Kaufman. A legend among birders, Kenn Kaufman hitchhiked back and forth across North America at age sixteen, traveling to see as many birds as he could. He is a field editor for *Audubon* and a regular contributor to every major birding magazine.

A Photographic Guide to North American Raptors by Brian K. Wheeler and William S. Clark may be of interest if you want to learn more about birds of prey. Raptors are not always easy to identify, and these two top experts provide an essential guide to variations in the species. The book contains over 300 photos allowing easier recognition of key identification points.

THE BLACK-BELLIED WHISTLING DUCK SPORTS A BEAUTIFUL RED BILL AND WHEN IN FLIGHT, IT'S HIGH PITCHED WHISTLES PIERCE THE SKIES.

The Art of Pishing: How to Attract Birds by Making Their Sounds (with Audio CD) by Pete Dunne is a fun book that explores how to attract birds by making precise and well-practiced hisses, whistles, chips, and squeals, along with some kisses and thumps. Dunne presents an illustrated workshop on the art of pishing.

Good Birders Don't Wear White, edited by Lisa White, contains fifty tips from top birders in North America. A delightful book, it offers light, sometimes humorous, essays ranging from bird feeding to pishing to birding with children. It is a book worth reading, if for nothing else but to get a look at birdwatching from the perspective of some talented birders.

Bird Finding Guides

The ABA publishes and distributes the *ABA Birdfinding Guide* series, which is widely recognized as setting the gold standard for site guides in North America. It features the best information available on bird distribution within "hot spot" areas of North America, such as Florida, Southeastern Arizona, Southern California, Alaska, and many other regions. Special features include annotated species lists, bar graphs representing seasonal distribution, and maps of key sites. The guides are written by expert birders from each region covered in the series and benefit greatly from the skills of a highly experienced editorial and map-making team. These guides are incredibly helpful when you are trying to find specific locations of birds.

Journal Publications

There are a number of scientific journals that deal with birds. These journal submissions are written by serious birders, wildlife ecologists, and professional and lay ornithologists. The journals are typically produced by the ornithological or scientific community and can be subscribed to as any magazine. While they are not written for the beginning birder, they do provide research information about birds that may interest a more advanced birder or someone involved with the conservation issues of birds.

Additionally, state ornithological societies often have their own journals, and the American Birding Association has a quarterly journal of ornithological record.

North American Birds (*NAB*) includes bird records, range extensions and contractions, population dynamics, and changes in migration patterns. *NAB* provides indispensable information for the serious birder. It is available by subscription separate from an ABA membership.

The Ornithological Council, a public information organization established and supported by eleven North American professional ornithological societies, posts

THE MARBLED GODWIT (FOREGROUND) FORAGES IN MUDFLATS AND IN MARSHES BY PROBING IN THE MUD WITH ITS LONG BILL.

information and society journal publications on the website Birdnet: (www.nmnh.si.edu/BIRDNET/mainindex.html)

BIRDING ONLINE

Birding online is just not the same as birding in the field. However, there are some great sites that can help you learn more about birds and improve your identification skills. Be careful as you search the web for information. You need to be sure that the source you are using as a reference is reliable. Not all information posted on a website is always accurate or true

The e-Nature Website (www.enature.com/fieldguides) is a good website for information about identification of birds as well as articles on other nature topics. The "Wildlife Guide" section includes birds, which are divided into categories such as wading birds, duck-like birds, hawks, and tree-clinging birds. These types are based on shared characteristics or relationships, and the silhouette illustration shows a representative species from each type.

E-MAIL STATE LISTSERVES ARE A GREAT WAY TO FIND OUT WHAT SPECIES OTHER BIRDWATCHERS ARE SEEING IN YOUR AREA.

You can view all the birds and scroll through the pictures, or you can do a search for a specific species. You can do an advanced search by basic type, color, size, habitat, and region and get close to finding the type of bird you may have seen.

The Birds of North America (BNA) Online (bna.birds.cornell.edu/BNA). A joint effort of the Cornell Lab of Ornithology and the American Ornithologists Union, the Birds of North America (BNA) Online is one of the best sites online. BNA Online is a reference and research tool that offers a wealth of ornithological information. It is a reference for basic biological information on North American birds for lay birders as well as professional ornithologists and ecologists. It provides detailed scientific information for each of the 716 species of birds nesting in the United States and Canada.

The print version of BNA, a ten-year project, was completed in 2002. It was conducted jointly by the American Ornithologists Union, the Cornell Lab of Ornithology, and the Academy of Natural Sciences. The contents are updated frequently with online-coordinated contributions from researchers, citizen scientists, and designated reviewers and editors. BNA Online is building image and video galleries showing behavior, habitats, nests, eggs, nestlings, and more. Each species will contain recordings of that bird's songs and calls, selected from the collection in Cornell's Macaulay Library of Natural Sounds. The BNA is a wonderful resource for any level of interest and is available as a subscription. It is well worth the investment.

BirdSource (www.birdsource.org) is a website developed and managed by the Cornell Lab of Ornithology and Audubon. BirdSource provides the technology that powers the Lab's citizen science projects. BirdSource also implements a variety of interactive online projects. This is a great way to bird online. You can learn more about this site in Chapter Nine.

eBird (ebird.org/content/index.html) is a continent-wide, year-round survey of North American birds. eBird is a way to help birders manage their lists and provides a rich source for basic information on bird abundance and distribution at a variety of spatial scales. Launched in 2002 by the Cornell Lab of Ornithology and National Audubon Society, eBird's goal is to maximize the utility and accessibility of the vast numbers of bird observations made each year by recreational and professional birdwatchers. State-of-the-art web technology provides the ability to track birds and share information with scientists, teachers, amateur naturalists, and other birders. A bonus of eBird is the ability to access the trail tracker, which tracks the specific location of a bird on a map. You can also manage your bird list on this site.

The American Birding Association (www.americanbirding.org/resources/mailinglists.html) The American Birding Association website has a very complete list of various listserves, including some outside North America. There are state listserves designed for birders to post and receive bird sightings from around the state. Many of these state listserves also function as a way to communicate bird conservation issues or calendars of events of bird festivals, bird club meetings, and other events that birdwatchers may be interested in attending. Listserves are a great way to find the birds and birders in your area. Be sure to check your area for a listserve and sign up to receive the postings. If you don't like getting lots of e-mails most listserves give you the option to view archived postings.

The Ornithological Records Committee Directory and Membership Lists (http://home.rconnect.com/~phertzel/brc/brc.htm). For those of you who want to hunt for rare birds or to know what people are seeing, check out the Ornithological Records Committee Directory and Membership Lists which track bird records. The avian record committees review and judge observational reports of rare or unusual birds for defined geographic or political jurisdictions. It is fun to visit the lists from time to time to see what discussions are taking place concerning rare and unusual birds. You can visit the home website and then connect to the area you are interested in knowing more about.

Have fun birding online but don't stay at your computer too long. Nothing replaces getting out into the field and enjoying the birds in person. Use the websites and resources to support your hobby of birdwatching and to help you enjoy the birds more.

GLOSSARY

adaptation: the ability that enables a species to adjust to a changing environment.

alarm call: the call a bird gives to signal danger.

aviary: an enclosure for captive birds. Aviaries can be part of a zoo, park or nature center.

aquatic: an organism living or growing in water.

asynchronous hatching: hatching that does not occur at the same time and may take place over two to three days.

banding: the placement of a band on a bird to track the bird's movement over time.

bill-sweeping: when birds sweep their bills back and forth at a feeder.

birdhouse: another name for a nest box.

birder: someone who watches birds

birdsong: the musical sound made by birds.

bottomland: low-lying land along a stream, river, or brook.

Breeding Bird Survey (BBS): a survey usually performed in June by volunteers. There are over 4000 bird counts and the data generates the BBS maps showing the breeding distribution of birds.

breeding cycle: the time period beginning at nest building through mating, egg laying and raising young, to the point of independence

brood: a nest of chicks. Some birds have one, two, or even three broods of chicks.

brushpile: a pile of branches that can provide shelter for birds.

caching: the storage of berries, seeds, and other food items in the crevices of bark, under leaves, or in cavities.

camouflage: having colors that enable a bird to blend with its habitat.

carnivorous: feeding on live or deceased animals.

cavity: a hole or opening in a tree trunk or limb usually used for building a nest.

cavity-nesting bird: a bird that nests inside a hole in a tree trunk, limb, or in a nest box.

checklist: a list of birds that are checked off once they are spotted by a birdwatcher.

Christmas Bird Count (CBC): A volunteer survey the week before or after Christmas. Birds are counted in an area with a 15-mile radius. The data is used to generate the CBC maps.

clutch: total number of eggs laid by a female bird in one nest.

colonial nesting: when the same species of birds nest in groups or colonies.

coniferous: evergreen trees such as pines, firs, and trees that do not lose their leaves.

contour feather: predominate feather type found on the body, wings, and tail of the bird.

crest: feathers that can create a tuft on the top of a bird's head.

crop: a sac inside a bird where its neck meets the body, which holds food before digestion.

deciduous: trees or bushes that lose their leaves seasonally or at a certain stage of development.

distraction display: a bird pretending to be hurt to lure predators away from their nest or young.

distribution: the geographic area(s) where a species of bird is found.

dimorphism: existing in two forms or two color forms.

dispersal: the movement of a young bird from the place where it hatches to the site where it breeds. Also the year-to-year

BAR-HEADED GEESE ARE FROM ASIA. THEY TEND TO MATE FOR LIFE AND BOTH PARENTS HELP CARE FOR THE YOUNG.

movement of an adult bird from one site to another.

diurnal: active in the day. Most birds are diurnal.

dominance: the ability of one bird to dominate the actions of another.

ecotourism: travel to areas where the purpose is to support natural areas.

edge effect: different habitats meeting at an edge. An example is woods and a field coming together.

egg dumping: occurs when a female lays eggs in the nest of another bird. Because this makes a clutch larger than normal, it typically reduces the success of all the birds surviving.

falconry: hunting with trained and captive falcons.

fecal sac: a clean mucous membrane containing the excrement of nestling birds.

fledge: when a young bird leaves the nest. These birds, called fledglings, will typically stay close to the nest for a day or two.

feathers: also called plumage, feathers cover a bird's body.

field marks: characteristics such as color, shape, or specific marking such as eye rings, wing bars, and breast stripes, which distinguish one species from another.

flock: a group of birds.

food chain: the interrelationships among animals and plants concerning food.

frugivorous: birds that feed primarily on fruit. Cedar waxwings are frugivorous birds.

grit: small pieces of rock, shell, or other hard substances that birds eat to help them digest other foods. Grit helps grind up

PROVIDING FOOD YEAR ROUND WILL ENTICE MANY DIFFERENT SPECIES TO YOUR YARD.

coarse vegetable matter.

habitat: the place where an animal or plant lives.

habitat fragmentation: a large piece of habitat that has been altered.

habitat selection: certain habitats that attract birds. Forests and wetlands are both examples of habitats that birds select.

hatch: to emerge from an egg, pupa, or chrysalis.

hatching: the moment an organism emerges from an egg, pupa, or chrysalis.

hatchling: a hatched bird still in the nest.

herbivorous: birds that primarily eat plants. Many ducks and geese are herbivores.

hoarding: behavior in which birds hide food in bark crevices and under leaves, moss, or lichen. Retrieval of food items is accidental, not memory-based.

hovering: a technique used to search for food. A bird remains stationary in mid air, rapidly flapping its wings over its prey.

introduced species: species released by humans. This can include reintroductions, transplants, restocked species, or accidental releases through escape.

incubation: birds sitting on eggs until they hatch.

insectivore: birds that eat mainly insects. Swallows are an example of an insectivorous bird.

irruption: a sudden movement of birds, usually large in number.

latitude: the south to north measurement of location.

life bird: a bird seen for the first time in the life of a birdwatcher.

life list: the list a birdwatcher keeps of the birds seen for the first time.

THE MOURNFUL SONG OF THE EASTERN MEADOWLARK IN WEEDY FIELDS AND MEADOWS IS A SPRINGTIME DELIGHT.

longitude: the east to west measurement of location.

mammal: warm-blooded animals that feed their young with milk provided by mammary glands.

migration: regular seasonal movements of birds between their breeding regions and wintering regions.

molt: the process of renewing part or all of the plumage by growing new feathers.

monogamy: the mating of a bird with only one individual at a time.

nest box: a box in which cavity-nesting birds can nest. Also called a birdhouse.

nestling: a young bird in the nest.

niche: the role a bird plays in the ecosystem, including what it eats and where it lives.

nocturnal: active in the night. Most owls are nocturnal.

non-native species: birds that have been released from or have escaped captivity. The English house sparrow is an example.

omnivorous: birds that eat anything considered edible. American crows are a good example.

ornithologist: a person who studies birds. Ornithology is the study of birds.

pair bond: two birds who have mated. This association can be short-term, lasting during egg-laying or the rearing of young, or a lifelong bond.

parasite: an organism that lives in or on and derives its nutriment from another organism.

pellets: regurgitated undigested food such as bones, feathers, and fur. Owl pellets can be found in areas where the birds roost after eating their prey.

IN PARKS AND PONDS ACROSS NORTH AMERICA, BIRDERS WILL SEE A WIDE VARIETY OF DOMESTIC AND WILD SPECIES OF DUCKS.

permanent resident: a species of bird that does not migrate and spends the entire year in the same region.

pishing: the ability to attract birds by pursing your lips or kissing your hand.

polygamy: one male bird mating with more than one female.

population: the total number of individuals of a single species living in a given area.

predation: preying on another animal for food.

preening: the process of cleaning and caring for feathers. Birds use their bills to adjust their feathers.

raptors: birds that prey on smaller birds and mammals. Raptors include hawks, eagles, falcons, and owls.

replacement clutch: when eggs are laid to replace a clutch in which none of the eggs hatched.

riparian: the area along banks of rivers and streams.

roost: a base or support on which birds rest, eat, or sleep.

snag: a standing dead tree or stump.

species: related organisms with common attributes, usually capable of interbreeding.

subspecies: a population within a species that shows variation.

synchronous hatching: hatching that occurs at the same time or nearly the same time, usually within one calendar day.

taxonomy: scientific naming of organisms and their classification.

wave: when a group of birds suddenly moves through an area, typically during migration and sometimes during or after a storm.

Binocular Features

TAKE THE TIME TO RESEARCH THE RIGHT OPTICS FOR YOU

BINOCULARS ARE LABELED WITH TWO NUMBERS SEPARATED BY AN "X." THE FIRST IS THE MAGNIFICATION; THE SECOND IS THE DIAMETER LENS.

BINOCULARS ARE EITHER TRULY WATERPROOF, WATER RESISTANT, AND/OR FOG PROOF. CHECK BEFORE YOU PURCHASE.

INSPECTING NECK STRAPS FOR WEAR AND TEAR WILL PREVENT ACCIDENTS AND FATIGUE PLUS RELIEVE STRAIN ON THE BACK.

PREMIUM BINOCULARS ARE MADE WITH THE HIGHEST QUALITY LENSES AND FEATURE ANTI-REFLECTION COATING. ADJUSTABLE CAPS PROTECT THE FRONT LENS.

POSITION THE BINOCULAR SO THE EYEPIECES LINE UP WITH YOUR EYES AND THEN ADJUST THE FOCUS WITH THE FOCUS WHEEL, SEEN HERE WITH + AND -.

THE DIOPTER ALLOWS FOR SEPARATE ADJUSTMENTS OF EACH INDIVIDUAL EYEPIECE. THIS WILL COMPENSATE FOR VISION VARIATIONS IN EACH EYE.

MOST MODELS ARE ARMORED WITH A RUBBERY MATERIAL DESIGNED TO WITHSTAND MOISTURE, ROUGH TREATMENT, AND TO HELP PROVIDE A SOLID GRIP.

CAMERA EYEPIECES FOR SPOTTING SCOPES COME IN SEVERAL DIFFERENT POSITIONS. SOME PROVIDE A STRAIGHT VIEW INTO THE BARREL OF THE SCOPE AND OTHERS ARE ANGLED. BOTH HAVE ADVANTAGES. USE OF A MODEST SCOPE WITH A DIGITAL CAMERA CAN PROVIDE MAGNIFICATION EQUAL TO A 1000 MM LENS.

BIBLIOGRAPHY

THERE ARE MANY ARTICLES, JOURNALS, SCIENTIFIC
PAPERS, BOOKS, AND WEB SITES THAT ARE WELL REGARDED
IN THE WORLD OF BIRDING, BUT OUR KEY RESOURCES
ARE LISTED BELOW

Identify Yourself, by Bill Thompson III. 2005. Houghton Mifflin Company. New York, New York.

American Bird Conservancy's All the Birds of North America, by Jack Griggs. 1997. Harper Resource. New York, New York.

The Practical Ornithologist, by John Gooders, and Scott Weidensaul. 1990. Simon & Schuster. New York, New York.

The Lives of North American Birds, by Kenn Kaufman. 1996. Houghton Mifflin Company. New York, New York.

Bird Conservation Alliance, facilitated by the American Bird Conservancy, www. birdconservationalliance.org.

Bird Studies Canada, www.bsc-eoc.org.

National Wildlife Federation, www.nwf.org.

Nature Canada, www.naturecanada.ca.

North American Bluebird Society, www. nabluebirdsociety.org.

Ornithological Council, www.nmnh. si.edu/BIRDNET.

Patuxent Wildlife Research Center, www. pwrc.usgs.gov/birds.

Partners in Flight, www.partnersinflight.org.

Fatal Light Awareness Program, www. flap.org.

The Bird Conservation Network, www. bcnbirds.org.

New York Audubon Society, www. nycaudubon.org.

The International Crane Foundation, www.savingcranes.org/species/whooping.cfm.

The Smithsonian Migratory Bird Center, www.nationalzoo.si.edu/Conservation AndScience/MigratoryBirds.

American Bird Conservancy, www. abcbirds.org.

The United States Fish and Wildlife Service, www.fws.gov/birds.

Ducks Unlimited, www.ducks.org.

Cornell Lab of Ornithology, www.birds. cornell.edu.

Birders' Exchange, www.americanbirding. org/bex/index.html.

Cats Indoors! Campaign/American Bird Conservancy, www.abcbirds.org/cats.

Whooping Crane Eastern Partnership, www.bringbackthecranes.org/index.html.

Operation Migration, www.operationmi gration.org.

Bahamas National Trust, www.thebaha masnationaltrust.org/partners.php.

BirdLife International, www.birdlife. org/action/science/sites/index.html.

Canada IBA, www.ibacanada.com.

National Audubon Society, www.audubon. org/bird/iba/index.html.

Park Flight Migratory Bird Program, www.nps.gov/oia/topics/flight.htm.

American Birding Association, www. americanbirding.org/resources/ shadecoffee/songbird.html.

National Audubon Society, www.audubon coffeeclub.com/shop/home.php.

Seattle Audubon/Northwest Shade Coffee, www.shadecoffee.org.

Smithsonian Migratory Bird Center, www. nationalzoo.si.edu/Conservationand Science/MigratoryBirds/Coffee/.

Avian Incident Monitoring System, www. abcbirds.org/aims/.

BirdLife International, www.birdlife.org.

Blue Ocean, www.blueocean.org.

ACKNOWLEDGMENTS
Alicia King

I wish to thank my husband, Raymond, for his undying love, bird watching companionship, and continuing support of my work. I also wish to thank my daughter, Kathleen Lich, and my stepson, Chris King, for sharing my passion, and for their continued support of my conservation efforts. Through the years I have met many great birders and have learned a lot about the value of birds in our environment. I wish to thank Dr. David Bonter of the Cornell Lab of Ornithology.

I have developed many friendships through birding and bird conservation, and appreciate the support these friends have given me, especially Scott Weidensaul, John Faaborg, Bill Thompson III, and Kenn Kaufman. I am very thankful to be working at the American Bird Conservancy, and thank my colleagues, George Wallace, Gavin Shire, Hana Young, Darin Schroeder, David Pashley, Hugo Arnal, and Paul Salaman. Special thanks to George Fenwick, President and CEO of the American Bird Conservancy, for his continued dedication to the conservation of birds throughout the Americas.

BAND-F Ltd., Bruce Curtis and f-stop Fitzgerald

We would like to thank Leigh and Perk Perkins and Tom Rosenbauer of The Orvis Company for their tremendous support, and Winnie Prentice, Barbara Harold, Bryan Trandem, Brad Springer, and Michelle Lancialtomare of Creative Publishing international for their vision in developing this book with us.

Thanks to Bill Pekala and Melissa DeBartolo of Nikon Professional Services, and Jon LaCorte of Nikon Sport Optics, for allowing us the use of lenses, 35mm and compact cameras, scopes, and binoculars.

Thanks to Visit Florida (www.visitflorida.com), the state tourism agency, especially Paul Kayemba and Cassie Henderson.

Thanks to Ranger Toni Westland of Ding Darling NWR, Nancy Hamilton, Director of Communications for Lee County Visitor & Convention Bureau out of Fort Myers, and Casey Bruni, Manager at the Babcock

GROOMING IS IMPORTANT BEHAVIOR TO SPECIES SUCH AS THE HAMMERKOP, FOUND IN SOUTH AFRICA.

Ranch & Cypress Lodge. Thanks to Becky Bovell and Rebecca Allen of Charlotte Harbor & the Gulf Islands Visitor's Bureau; Gregg Klowden and Paul Holmes of the Peace River Audubon Society; and Missy Christie, Charlotte County Environmental Specialist. Thanks to the Peace River Wildlife Center. While in Charlotte County, generous accommodations were granted by Best Western Waterfront, Fishermen's Village, Harbor Pointe Condominium Resort, and Palm Island Resort. Additional accommodations were provided by Rob DeCastro and Jane Watkins, of the Lemon Tree Inn, Naples; Sasha Hlozek at the famous Cheeca Lodge in Islamorada; the Spring Hill Suites in Tampa; the Innisbrook Resort & Golf Club in Palm Harbor; Cathleen Casper at Key West's magnificent Casa Marine Resort; and The Point in Saranac, New York.

Thanks to David Ferrara and Jill Revelle for photography access to Busch Gardens Africa,

THE EURASIAN COLLARED-DOVE'S RANGE IS SPREADING ACROSS NORTH AMERICA. IT CAN BE FOUND IN BOTH URBAN AND RURAL AREAS AND IS CONSIDERED A POPULAR PET.

National Estuarine Research Reserve, host of the annual Southwest Florida Birding Festival each year; Everglades National Park; Big Cypress National Preserve; and especially Florida Fish & Wildlife Conservation Commission, developers of the Great Florida Birding Trail. The Theodore Roosevelt Bird Sanctuary in New York was a tremendous resource.

Special thanks to Airtran (www.airtran. com) for truly excellent airline transportation. Their motto is: "Go. There's nothing stopping you."

*air*Tran™

For great help photographing birds on the water, thanks to Capt. Mark Ward of Everglades Angler, Capt. Bruce Hitchcock in Chokoloskee, FL, Capt. Dan Malzone, Capt. Ralph Allen, and Capt. Les Hill. And Capt. Les Hill of Charlotte County, Florida.

Thanks to Andy Flynn, Senior Public Information Specialist; and Lydia Wright, Adirondack Park Naturalist at the New York State Adirondack Park Agency Visitor Interpretive Center at Paul Smiths. And to Margaret Marchuk, Director of Media Relations, Lake Placid Essex County Visitors Bureau.

Special thanks to Judith, Weston, and Genni Minissali for watching the birds with us; Bill and Eleanor Marr for identifying and photographing birds for us; Stephanie Lora for her professionalism and undying patience; project manager Karen Jones; editorial

in Tampa, Florida. Their aviary is filled with some of the world's most beautiful birds. Also to Rachel Nelson at Tampa's Lowry Park Zoo, and Executive Director Brian Holley at Naples Botanical Garden, for allowing access to their wonderful aviary facilities.

There are many local and state tourism agencies that were extremely helpful in creating this book: Bill AuCoin of AuCoin Associates Inc., in St. Petersburg /Clearwater; James Raulerson of St. Petersburg/Clearwater Convention and Visitors Bureau (CVB); Lisa Humphrey, Public Relations (PR) Representative for the Tampa Bay CVB; Josie Gulliksen from Newman PR; Milt Adams from the Paul Smiths Adirondack Park Visitor Interpretive Center; Jonell Moodys, PR & Communications Manager of Naples, Marco Island, Everglades CVB; Rookery Bay assistant Mie Kingsley; plus Ben Talutto and Barbara Piombino, our neighborhood birding consultants. Also Julie Sampson, Sheila Sampson, Kathy Gustafson, Rachel Gustafson, Neil Gustafson, Carrie Corrigan, Colleen Corrigan, Stella Miller, Lorraine Gilligan, Hannah Arnholt, Don Kavanaugh, and Billy Finigan.

ABOUT THE AUTHORS

Alicia King

Alicia King is the director of the Bird Conservation Alliance at the American Bird Conservancy. A songbird rehabilitator and bird bander, she has worked as a naturalist in Florida, where she created and presented environmental educational programs. King serves on the Association of Field Ornithologists Council and on the boards of Operation Migration and the Ornithological Council. She is also a member of the American Ornithologists Union Committee on Conservation.

King was a guest host on the Connecticut PBS television program *BirdWatch,* and hosted the *Bird Feature* segment on *Discover the Wild* for Wyoming PBS. She also created and hosted *For the Birds* for a CBS Indianapolis affiliate. King lectures and presents workshops on bird identification, conservation issues, habitat creation, and whooping crane reintroduction. Her organizational workshops include topics such as how to acquire publicity, volunteer acquisition and retention, and conservation.

f-stop Fitzgerald

f-stop Fitzgerald is a bestselling author, international photographer, and President of BAND-F Ltd., a book packaging company. Fitzgerald has extensive expertise in the publishing, printing, and photography industries, and his photography has been featured in over one hundred magazines, from *Rolling Stone* to *GQ.* His bestselling book collaboration with Stephen King, *Nightmares in the Sky,* sold over 180,000 copies. Other books include *The Mighty Fallen* with Larry Bond, *Pillars of the Almighty* with Ken Follett, *The Elements of Fly Fishing,* and *Not Fade Away: The Online World Remembers Jerry Garcia.* In addition to his tenure as co-founder of BAND-F Ltd., he has also held executive positions as senior director of operations at Avalon Publishing and C.O.O. of Hylas Publishing.

Bruce Curtis

Bruce Curtis has chronicled many of the significant events of the last decades of the twentieth century as photographer for *Time, LIFE,* and *Sports Illustrated.* A visual historian, some of his photographs are included in the Smithsonian Institution's permanent collection. Curtis has won 18 awards for his photography, including Photographer of the Year from the Overseas Press Club for his work in Vietnam. He is the exclusive photographer of more than 25 books including *The Art of Fly Fishing: An Illustrated History of Rods, Reels, and Favorite Flies;* and *The Art of Golf Antiques: An Illustrated History of Clubs, Balls, and Accessories.* Forthcoming titles include *Golfing for Seniors, The Wisdom of Iggy,* and three gardening books.

LIFE LIST

THE FOLLOWING LIST IS PROVIDED TO HELP YOU KEEP TRACK OF SOME OF THE BIRDS YOU MAY FIND ON BIRDWATCHING TRIPS. IT IS GROUPED AS FAMILIES WHERE APPROPRIATE, HOWEVER, IT DOES NOT FOLLOW STRICT SCIENTIFIC GUIDELINES. USE YOUR FIELD GUIDE AS A CROSS REFERENCE.

Bittern
☐ American Bittern _____
☐ Least Bittern _____

Blackbird
☐ Red-winged Blackbird _____
☐ Yellow-headed Blackbird _____
☐ Brown-headed Cowbird _____

Bluebirds
☐ Eastern Bluebird _____
☐ Western Bluebird _____
☐ Mountain Bluebird _____

Chickadee/Titmouse
☐ Black-capped Chickadee _____
☐ Carolina Chickadee _____
☐ Tufted Titmouse _____

Cormorant
☐ Great Cormorant _____
☐ Double-crested Cormorant _____

Cuckoo
☐ Black-billed Cuckoo _____
☐ Yellow-billed Cuckoo _____

Grackle
☐ Boat-tailed Grackle _____
☐ Common Grackle _____

Duck
☐ Wood Duck _____
☐ Green-winged Teal _____
☐ American Black Duck _____
☐ Mallard _____
☐ Northern Pintail _____

- ☐ Blue-winged Teal _____
- ☐ Northern Shoveler _____
- ☐ Eurasian Wigeon _____
- ☐ American Wigeon _____
- ☐ Canvasback _____
- ☐ Redhead _____
- ☐ Ring-necked Duck _____
- ☐ Common Goldeneye _____
- ☐ Bufflehead _____
- ☐ Hooded Merganser _____
- ☐ Common Merganser _____
- ☐ Red-breasted Merganser _____
- ☐ Ruddy Duck _____
- ☐ Fulvous Whistling-Duck _____

Eagle
- ☐ Bald Eagle _____
- ☐ Golden Eagle _____

Egret
- ☐ Great Egret _____
- ☐ Snowy Egret _____
- ☐ Cattle Egret _____

Falcon
- ☐ American Kestrel _____
- ☐ Peregrine Falcon _____

Finch
- ☐ Purple Finch _____
- ☐ House Finch _____
- ☐ Red Crossbill _____
- ☐ Common Redpoll _____
- ☐ Pine Siskin _____
- ☐ American Goldfinch _____

Flycatcher
- ☐ Olive-sided Flycatcher _____
- ☐ Eastern Wood-Pewee _____
- ☐ Yellow-bellied Flycatcher _____
- ☐ Acadian Flycatcher _____
- ☐ Great Crested Flycatcher _____
- ☐ Eastern Phoebe _____

Goatsuckers
- ☐ Common Nighthawk _____
- ☐ Chuck-will's Widow _____
- ☐ Chimney Swift _____

Goose
- ☐ Greater Snow Goose _____
- ☐ Canada Goose _____
- ☐ Ross' Goose _____

Gulls
- ☐ Laughing Gull _____
- ☐ Black-headed Gull _____
- ☐ Ring-billed Gull _____
- ☐ Herring Gull _____
- ☐ Lesser Black-backed Gull _____

Grosbeak
- ☐ Evening Grosbeak _____
- ☐ Rose-breasted Grosbeak _____
- ☐ Cardinal _____
- ☐ Indigo Bunting _____

Grebe
- ☐ Pied-billed Grebe _____
- ☐ Horned Grebe _____
- ☐ Red-necked Grebe _____

THE AFRICAN YELLOW-BILLED DUCK IS FAIRLY COMMON IN PARTS OF EAST AND SOUTH AFRICA.

Hawk

- ☐ Northern Harrier _____
- ☐ Sharp-shinned Hawk _____
- ☐ Cooper's Hawk _____
- ☐ Red-shouldered Hawk _____
- ☐ Red-tailed Hawk _____
- ☐ Rough-legged Hawk _____
- ☐ Broad-winged Hawk _____
- ☐ Swainson's Hawk _____

Heron

- ☐ Great Blue Heron _____
- ☐ Little Blue Heron _____
- ☐ Tricolored Heron _____
- ☐ Green Heron _____
- ☐ Black-crowned Night-Heron _____
- ☐ Yellow-crowned Night-Heron _____

Hummingbird

- ☐ Anna's Hummingbird _____

- ☐ Ruby-throated Hummingbird _____
- ☐ Rufous Hummingbird _____

Ibis

- ☐ White Ibis _____
- ☐ Glossy Ibis _____

Jay/crow

- ☐ Blue Jay _____
- ☐ Steller's Jay _____
- ☐ American Crow _____
- ☐ Fish Crow _____

Kingbird

- ☐ Western Kingbird _____
- ☐ Eastern Kingbird _____

Kingfisher

- ☐ Belted Kingfisher _____
- ☐ Green Kingfisher _____

Kinglet/Gnatcatcher

- ☐ Golden-crowned Kinglet _____
- ☐ Ruby-crowned Kinglet _____
- ☐ Blue-gray Gnatcatcher _____

Loon

- ☐ Red-throated Loon _____
- ☐ Common Loon _____

Mockingbird/Thrasher/Catbird

- ☐ Gray Catbird _____
- ☐ Northern Mockingbird _____
- ☐ Brown Thrasher _____

Nuthatch/Creeper

- ☐ Red-breasted Nuthatch _____
- ☐ White-breasted Nuthatch _____
- ☐ Brown-headed Nuthatch _____
- ☐ Brown Creeper _____

Oriole

- ☐ Baltimore Oriole _____
- ☐ Orchard Oriole _____
- ☐ Bullock's Oriole _____

Owl

- ☐ Barn Owl _____
- ☐ Barred Owl _____
- ☐ Eastern Screech-Owl _____
- ☐ Western Screech-Owl _____
- ☐ Great Horned Owl _____
- ☐ Snowy Owl _____

Pelican

- ☐ American White Pelican _____
- ☐ Brown Pelican _____

Plover/Killdeer

- ☐ Black-bellied Plover _____
- ☐ American Golden-Plover _____
- ☐ Wilson's Plover _____
- ☐ Semipalmated Plover _____
- ☐ Piping Plover _____
- ☐ Killdeer _____

Sandpipers

- ☐ Solitary Sandpiper _____
- ☐ Spotted Sandpiper _____
- ☐ Upland Sandpiper _____
- ☐ Semipalmated Sandpiper _____
- ☐ Western Sandpiper _____
- ☐ Least Sandpiper _____
- ☐ White-rumped Sandpiper _____
- ☐ Willet _____
- ☐ Marbled Godwit _____
- ☐ Ruddy Turnstone _____
- ☐ Red Knot _____
- ☐ Sanderling _____
- ☐ Wilson's Phalarope _____

Skimmer

- ☐ Black Skimmer _____

Sparrow

- ☐ American Tree Sparrow _____
- ☐ Chipping Sparrow _____
- ☐ Field Sparrow _____
- ☐ Fox Sparrow _____
- ☐ Song Sparrow _____
- ☐ White-throated Sparrow _____
- ☐ White-crowned Sparrow _____
- ☐ Dark-eyed Junco _____

THE JOYS OF BIRDING ARE OFTEN EXPRESSED THROUGH ART.

Stilt/Avocet
- ☐ Black-necked Stilt _____
- ☐ American Avocet _____

Swallow
- ☐ Tree Swallow _____
- ☐ Bank Swallow _____
- ☐ Barn Swallow _____
- ☐ Purple Martin _____

Swan
- ☐ Tundra Swan _____
- ☐ Mute Swan _____

Tanager
- ☐ Summer Tanager _____
- ☐ Scarlet Tanager _____

Terns
- ☐ Caspian Tern _____
- ☐ Royal Tern _____
- ☐ Sandwich Tern _____
- ☐ Common Tern _____
- ☐ Least Tern _____
- ☐ Black Tern _____

Thrush
- ☐ Swainson's Thrush _____
- ☐ Hermit Thrush _____
- ☐ Wood Thrush _____
- ☐ American Robin _____

Vulture
- ☐ Black Vulture _____
- ☐ Turkey Vulture _____

ONCE AN ENDANGERED SPECIES, PELICAN POPULATIONS IN THE UNITED STATES ARE NOW STABLE OR RISING.

Warbler

☐ Blue-winged Warbler _____
☐ Golden-winged Warbler _____
☐ Tennessee Warbler _____
☐ Nashville Warbler _____
☐ Northern Parula _____
☐ Yellow Warbler _____
☐ Chestnut-sided Warbler _____
☐ Magnolia Warbler _____
☐ Cape May Warbler _____
☐ Black-throated Blue Warbler _____
☐ Yellow-rumped Warbler _____
☐ Black-throated Green Warbler _____
☐ Blackburnian Warbler _____
☐ Yellow-throated Warbler _____

☐ Pine Warbler _____
☐ Prairie Warbler _____
☐ Palm Warbler _____
☐ Bay-breasted Warbler _____
☐ Blackpoll Warbler _____
☐ Cerulean Warbler _____
☐ Black-and-white Warbler _____
☐ American Redstart _____
☐ Prothonotary Warbler _____
☐ Worm-eating Warbler _____
☐ Swainson's Warbler _____
☐ Ovenbird _____
☐ Kentucky Warbler _____
☐ Connecticut Warbler _____
☐ Common Yellowthroat _____
☐ Hooded Warbler _____
☐ Wilson's Warbler _____
☐ Canada Warbler _____

Vireo

☐ White-eyed Vireo _____
☐ Red-eyed Vireo _____

Waterthrush

☐ Northern Waterthrush _____
☐ Louisiana Waterthrush _____

Woodpecker

☐ Red-headed Woodpecker _____
☐ Red-bellied Woodpecker _____
☐ Yellow-bellied Sapsucker _____
☐ Downy Woodpecker _____
☐ Hairy Woodpecker _____
☐ Northern Flicker _____
☐ Pileated Woodpecker _____

Wren

- ☐ Cactus Wren _____
- ☐ Carolina Wren _____
- ☐ House Wren _____
- ☐ Winter Wren _____

Yellowlegs

- ☐ Greater Yellowlegs _____
- ☐ Lesser Yellowlegs _____

Miscellaneous Birds

- ☐ American Coot _____
- ☐ American Oystercatcher _____
- ☐ American Woodcock _____
- ☐ Bobolink _____
- ☐ Cedar Waxwing _____

- ☐ Common Moorhen _____
- ☐ Common Snipe _____
- ☐ Eastern Meadowlark _____
- ☐ Eastern Towhee _____
- ☐ English House Sparrow _____
- ☐ European Starling _____
- ☐ Horned Lark _____
- ☐ Northern Bobwhite _____
- ☐ Northern Gannet _____
- ☐ Mourning Dove _____
- ☐ Osprey _____
- ☐ Purple Gallinule _____
- ☐ Rock Dove (Pigeon) _____
- ☐ Sora _____
- ☐ Yellow-breasted Chat _____

THE FEMALE RED-WINGED BLACKBIRD IS MAINLY A BROWNISH COLOR WITH A WHITE EYE STREAK. THOUGH THEY PREFER CATTAIL MARSHES FOR NESTING, BLACKBIRD PAIRS ALSO ROOST IN BUSHES AND TREES.

INDEX

THE BOLD ENTRIES SIGNIFY
A PHOTOGRAPH ON THE PAGE.

NOTES

PHOTO CREDITS